MW01503628

Unlock The
Healing Power
of the
VAGUS NERVE

A Somatic Approach to treating trauma,
anxiety and depression

Tatiana De Oliveira Pegado

Table Of Contents

Introduction

I have struggled with anxiety and depression most of my life, feeling trapped in a cycle of overwhelming emotions and physiological distress. It wasn't until I discovered the vagus nerve's power that my life changed. Through targeted exercises and a deeper understanding of my body's internal regulation system, I found a path to healing and resilience.

The vagus nerve, a long, wandering nerve that extends from the brainstem to the abdomen, plays a crucial role in our emotional and physical well-being. This remarkable nerve influences our heart rate, digestion, and immune response. Still, most importantly, it acts as a bridge between our body and brain, helping to regulate our stress response and emotional balance.

For those struggling with trauma, anxiety, and depression, understanding the vagus nerve can be a game-changer. When we experience chronic stress or trauma, our vagus nerve can become dysregulated, leading to a heightened stress response and difficulty returning to a state of calm. This dysregulation lies at the heart of many mental health challenges, perpetuating a cycle of emotional distress and physiological imbalance.

My name is Tatiana, and I am a Sacred Geometry Energy Healing Practitioner. As a passionate advocate for mental health and well-being, I have witnessed firsthand the transformative power of working with the vagus nerve. My journey of healing and growth has been deeply influenced by the science of polyvagal theory and the practical applications of vagus nerve stimulation. This personal experience, extensive research, and clinical expertise have inspired me to write this book.

Recent scientific studies have shed light on the profound impact of vagus nerve stimulation on mental health outcomes. Research has shown that targeted exercises and techniques designed to activate the vagus nerve can help reduce anxiety, alleviate symptoms of depression, and promote emotional regulation. These findings offer hope and validation for those seeking a somatic approach to healing.

In the following pages, you will embark on a journey of discovery, learning about the intricacies of the vagus nerve and its role in your mental and physical health. Through accessible explanations, practical exercises, and real-life case studies, you will gain the knowledge and tools necessary to harness the power of your vagus nerve.

As you progress through the book, you will learn how to recognize signs of vagal dysregulation in your body and develop a personalized toolkit of techniques to promote vagal tone and emotional resilience. You will discover the profound connection between your mind and body and learn how to cultivate a sense of safety and calm from within.

This book invites you to actively participate in your healing and well-being. By engaging with the material and applying the strategies presented, you can transform your relationship with stress, anxiety, and depression. You will learn to listen to your body's innate wisdom and develop more self-awareness and self-regulation.

The journey of healing through the vagus nerve is one of empowerment and self-discovery. As you turn the pages, I encourage you to approach the material with curiosity, compassion, and a willingness to explore new possibilities. Remember, the power to heal and thrive lies within you. By understanding and nurturing your vagus nerve, you are taking a significant step toward reclaiming your emotional and physical well-being.

Together, let us embark on this transformative journey, unlocking the potential of your vagus nerve and paving the way for a life of greater resilience, joy, and inner peace.

Chapter 1:

UNDERSTANDING THE VAGUS NERVE

In a bustling city, amidst the noise and haste, a quiet revolution was taking place within the walls of a small clinic. Here, a woman named Emily found solace from the relentless grip of anxiety that had shadowed her for years. The key to her newfound peace lay not in a bottle of pills or a therapist's couch but in the gentle stimulation of a nerve that had been silently orchestrating the rhythms of her body all along. The often-overlooked vagus nerve emerged as the cornerstone of her healing journey, providing a tangible connection between her physical and emotional states. This chapter will guide you through the remarkable anatomy and pathways of the vagus nerve, revealing how this intricate network influences vital bodily functions and potentially transforms mental health.

1.1 The Vagus Nerve Unveiled: Anatomy and Pathways

The vagus nerve, formally known as the tenth cranial nerve or CN X, is a crucial component of the parasympathetic nervous system, the part of our autonomic nervous system responsible for rest and recovery processes. Originating from the medulla oblongata, a region at the base of your brainstem, the vagus nerve extends like a vast network of communication lines, reaching into the depths of your neck, thorax, and abdomen. This nerve is aptly named the "wandering" nerve, as it meanders through your body with a complex and far-reaching presence. It travels within the carotid sheath, alongside the jugular vein and carotid artery, weaving through your body to establish vital connections. As it courses through the thorax, the right vagus nerve forms the posterior vagal trunk while the left forms the anterior, contributing to intricate networks such as the esophageal plexus and cardiac branches. These pathways are anatomical marvels and lifelines that sustain essential bodily functions.

The bifurcation of the vagus nerve is where its profound impact truly unfolds. Upon reaching various organs, it branches extensively, establishing connections with the heart, lungs, and digestive system. This branching allows the vagus nerve to exert its regulatory influence on heart rate and digestive processes. The parasympathetic functions of the vagus nerve involve calming and restorative actions that counterbalance the stress-induced responses of its sympathetic counterpart. As it wraps around the heart, it plays a pivotal role in heart rate modulation, acting as a natural pacemaker that helps maintain a steady, calming rhythm. Its influence extends to the lungs, where it regulates breathing patterns, and to the digestive system, where it promotes peristalsis and the secretion of digestive enzymes, ensuring smooth and efficient digestion.

In parasympathetic functions, the vagus nerve is akin to a maestro conducting an orchestra of physiological responses, each attuned to the body's need for restoration. One of its most profound roles is regulating heart rate, ensuring the heart beats with a gentle, rhythmic cadence. This regulation is not merely a matter of maintaining homeostasis but is integral to how we experience stress and relaxation. When the vagus nerve functions optimally, it acts as a calming force, reducing stress responses and promoting relaxation. The digestive system orchestrates the seamless food transition through the gastrointestinal tract, facilitating nutrient absorption and digestive efficiency. This calming influence also extends to the immune system, where the vagus nerve acts as a mediator, tempering inflammatory responses and promoting balance.

The vagus nerve's impact on the body's "rest and digest" state is profound, offering a sanctuary from the storm of stress and anxiety. The vagus nerve helps shift the body from heightened alertness to relaxation and recovery by activating the parasympathetic response. This shift is a physiological change and a profoundly transformative experience that can alter how you perceive and respond to the world around you. Reducing stress responses facilitated by the vagus nerve is a cornerstone of mental health, providing a foundation for emotional resilience and stability. Understanding and working with your vagus nerve can unlock a world of healing possibilities, offering a path to improved well-being and a renewed sense of calm in the face of life's challenges.

1.2 The Autonomic Nervous System: A Gateway to Healing

The autonomic nervous system (ANS) operates as the body's automatic pilot, managing involuntary functions that are crucial for survival. It comprises two primary branches: the sympathetic and parasympathetic nervous systems. Think of the sympathetic system as the body's accelerator; it prepares us for action by increasing heart rate, directing blood flow to muscles, and releasing adrenaline. This is the "fight or flight" response—our instinctual reaction to perceived threats. On the other hand, the parasympathetic system acts as the brake, promoting relaxation and recovery. It encourages the body to "rest and digest," slowing the heart rate, enhancing digestion, and facilitating healing. Together, these systems create a dynamic balance, allowing us to adapt to the demands of the environment while maintaining internal stability.

Focusing on the parasympathetic nervous system profoundly impacts healing and recovery. This branch nurtures a state of calm and restoration, crucial for sustaining health and well-being. It fosters processes that repair tissues, reduce inflammation, and conserve energy when activated. Consider the soothing sensation of sinking into a warm bath after a long day. Your heart rate slows, breathing deepens, and muscles relax—all thanks to the parasympathetic system at work. The regeneration it supports is not just physical; it extends to emotional well-being by promoting a sense of safety and tranquility. This restorative capacity is vital in counteracting the wear and tear of daily stressors, making it an integral part of sustaining mental health.

The vagus nerve is a critical conduit within the ANS, orchestrating the balance between these two branches. It acts as a mediator, ensuring that neither the sympathetic nor the parasympathetic system dominates excessively. In moments of stress or anxiety, the vagus nerve helps recalibrate the system, steering it back toward equilibrium. This interplay resembles a seesaw, where the vagus nerve maintains a delicate balance, preventing either side from tipping too far. When the vagus nerve functions optimally, it supports resilience, enabling the body to recover from stress swiftly and return to equilibrium. Its regulatory role is fundamental in preserving homeostasis, providing a buffer against the destabilizing effects of chronic stress.

Stimulating the vagus nerve can be a powerful tool for autonomic regulation, offering therapeutic potential in mental health care. Techniques activating the vagus nerve, such as deep breathing, meditation, and cold exposure, can reduce anxiety and stress. For instance, slow, diaphragmatic breathing can engage the vagus nerve, triggering a calming response that lowers heart rate and eases tension. This activation mitigates immediate stress and enhances the body's ability to manage future stressors. By fostering a state of relaxation, vagal stimulation supports emotional regulation, helping individuals navigate the challenges of trauma, anxiety, and depression with greater ease.

Imagine a scenario where someone faces an overwhelming workload and tight deadlines. The stress response kicks in, my heart racing, and thoughts spiraling. Regular vagal stimulation can provide the tools to counteract this response, promoting calm and clarity. By integrating these practices into daily life, individuals can cultivate a resilient nervous system, one that is equipped to handle stress without being consumed by it. The potential for healing through vagus nerve stimulation extends beyond temporary relief, offering a pathway to lasting mental health improvements. As we explore this intricate system, it becomes clear that the autonomic nervous system and the vagus nerve are not just physiological components but gateways to more profound healing and well-being.

1.3 Vagal Tone: Measuring the Unseen

Vagal tone is an often understated yet significant measure of autonomic nervous system health. It represents the activity of the vagus nerve, providing a window into how our bodies respond to stress and maintain balance. At its core, vagal tone reflects the body's ability to regulate physiological functions, particularly heart rate and emotional stability. It serves as an indicator of how well your body can shift between states of excitement and relaxation. High vagal tone is associated with a robust ability to manage stress, showcasing a capacity for resilience and adaptability. This concept becomes particularly tangible when we consider its correlation with heart rate variability (HRV), a measure of the variation in time between heartbeats. HRV is a proxy for vagal tone, offering insights into the body's stress response system. When your HRV is high, it suggests a healthy vagal tone, indicating that your body is adept at transitioning between different states of activity and rest. This flexibility is crucial for managing stress and emotional challenges effectively.

Understanding one's vagal tone involves exploring a variety of assessment methods. Heart rate monitors, for example, provide real-time data that can illuminate the nuances of your autonomic nervous system's functioning. Through these devices, you can track changes in HRV as you engage in different activities, offering a glimpse into how your body responds to stressors throughout the day. Another method, respiratory sinus arrhythmia, examines the natural variation in heart rate that occurs during breathing. By analyzing this aspect of your respiration, you can gain invaluable insights into your vagal tone. These assessments are not just clinical metrics but tools of empowerment, enabling you to understand your body's current state and potential for improvement.

The relationship between high vagal tone and mental health is profound. A higher vagal tone is often synonymous with greater emotional regulation, improving mood stability. When your vagal tone is high, it acts as a buffer against the volatility of emotional fluctuations, providing a stabilizing foundation that can help weather the storms of anxiety and depression. Imagine the calm that follows a deep breath during a moment of stress; that's the vagus nerve at work, gently guiding you back to a state of balance. Enhanced vagal tone translates to a more resilient emotional state, empowering you to face life's challenges with confidence and composure.

Practical exercises and lifestyle changes offer accessible pathways for those seeking to improve their vagal tone. Deep breathing exercises stand out as a simple yet powerful tool. You can activate the vagus nerve by taking slow, deliberate breaths, promoting a sense of calm and relaxation. Regular practice of such exercises can condition your body to respond more effectively to stress, gradually enhancing your vagal tone over time. Activities like yoga and meditation can also bolster these efforts, providing holistic benefits that extend beyond the physiological to embrace emotional and mental well-being. These practices foster an environment where the vagus nerve can thrive, nurturing a balance that supports overall health.

Incorporating small changes into daily life can have a profound impact. For instance, taking a few moments each day for focused deep breathing, especially during stressful times, can reinforce the calming effects of a healthy vagal tone. Picture yourself in a crowded subway, feeling the anxiety rise as the crowd jostles you. A few deep breaths can transform the chaos into a manageable situation, illustrating the power of the vagus nerve in real time. By prioritizing these practices, you cultivate a lifestyle that supports your nervous system and enhances your overall quality of life.

1.4 Neuroscience of Emotion Regulation: The Vagus Connection

The vagus nerve plays an intriguing role in emotional regulation, acting as a conductor within the intricate symphony of our brain's emotional centers. This nerve extends its influence to the prefrontal cortex and the amygdala, two critical regions involved in processing emotions and orchestrating responses to stress. The prefrontal cortex, located at the front of the brain, is often associated with higher-order functions like decision-making and impulse control. Meanwhile, the amygdala, nestled deeper within the brain's structure, is the epicenter of emotional reactions, particularly those related to fear and anxiety. The vagus nerve is a bridge, facilitating communication between these areas and influencing how we perceive and respond to emotional stimuli. By modulating signals between the prefrontal cortex and the amygdala, the vagus nerve helps regulate emotional responses, allowing for more measured reactions to stressors and challenges.

Neuroplasticity, the brain's remarkable ability to reorganize itself by forming new neural connections, is a key player in vagal stimulation. Effectively rewiring emotional responses over time. This brain malleability means individuals can enhance their capacity for emotional regulation with consistent practice. By stimulating the vagus nerve, we can influence the brain's plasticity, encouraging healthier pathways for processing emotions. This not only enhances our ability to manage stress and anxiety but also fosters a resilient mindset. Neuroplasticity offers a hopeful perspective on mental health, suggesting that even entrenched patterns of emotional reactivity can be reshaped with intentional effort and practice.

Scientific studies have illuminated the connection between vagal tone and emotional health, providing a robust foundation for understanding its impact. Research has shown that higher vagal tone correlates with reduced anxiety and improved emotional regulation. For instance, a study published in the Journal of Clinical Psychology found that individuals with higher vagal tone exhibited more excellent emotional stability and resilience in the face of stress. These findings underscore the importance of vagal tone as a marker of emotional health, suggesting that by enhancing vagal tone, individuals can experience a reduction in anxiety and an overall improvement in emotional well-being. The implications of this research are profound, offering a tangible target for those seeking to enhance their mental health through somatic practices.

Practical applications for enhancing emotional regulation through vagal stimulation are accessible and valuable. Mindfulness practices, which emphasize present-moment awareness and non-judgmental observation of thoughts and feelings, can be particularly beneficial. By incorporating mindfulness techniques such as meditation and deep breathing, individuals can activate the vagus nerve and promote a state of calm and balance. For example, practicing mindful breathing—taking slow, deliberate breaths while focusing on the sensations of inhalation and exhalation—can engage the vagus nerve, reducing stress and enhancing emotional regulation. These practices are simple to implement and offer cumulative benefits over time, making them valuable tools for managing anxiety and fostering emotional resilience.

Imagine a person facing a stressful situation, such as preparing for an important presentation. The heart races, breathing quickens, and anxiety looms large. By employing mindfulness techniques, such as taking a moment to breathe deeply and ground oneself in the present, the vagus nerve can be engaged to calm the body's stress response. This not only aids in reducing immediate anxiety but also builds a foundation for more adaptive emotional reactions in the future. With regular practice, these techniques can become intuitive responses to stress, empowering individuals to navigate life's challenges with greater ease and composure. Engaging with the vagus nerve through mindful practices offers a path to enhanced emotional regulation, providing a framework for improved mental health.

1.5 Understanding the Polyvagal Theory: Beyond Basics

The polyvagal theory, developed by Dr. Stephen Porges, offers a profound insight into the workings of our nervous system and its impact on behavior and social engagement. This theory highlights the vagus nerve's intricate role in shaping our interactions with the world. At its core, the polyvagal theory reveals that our nervous system is not solely about survival but connection. The vagus nerve mediates our internal emotions and external social behaviors with its ability to influence our physiological states. This connection forms the basis of what Dr. Porges calls the "social engagement system," a concept that explains how we communicate, connect, and create bonds with others. The social engagement system is a biological mechanism that allows us to feel safe and engage with others meaningfully. When the vagus nerve is in optimal function, it supports our ability to read social cues, maintain eye contact, and express emotions through facial expressions and vocal tone. This system underpins our capacity for empathy and compassion, essential components for building healthy relationships and communities.

The polyvagal theory describes three distinct neural circuits that govern our responses to the environment: immobilization, mobilization, and social engagement. Each circuit represents a different adaptive response to perceived safety or threat. The immobilization circuit, often associated with the "freeze" response, is activated when we feel overwhelmed or trapped, leading to a state of shutdown or dissociation. This response, deeply rooted in our evolutionary history, can manifest as a protective mechanism during extreme stress or trauma. The mobilization circuit, linked to the "fight or flight" response, prepares us for action in the face of danger. It heightens alertness and readiness, enabling us to confront or escape threats. This circuit, while necessary for survival, can become chronically activated in individuals with anxiety disorders, leading to persistent states of hyperarousal.

The social engagement circuit, facilitated by the vagus nerve, is the most intriguing aspect of the polyvagal theory. This circuit supports behaviors that foster connection and safety, allowing us to engage socially and form relationships. When activated, it promotes a sense of calm and cooperation, encouraging prosocial behaviors and emotional bonding. The interplay between these circuits is dynamic, with the vagus nerve acting as a regulator that helps us transition smoothly between different states, depending on the context. Understanding this balance is crucial in addressing trauma, anxiety, and depression, as it provides insight into how our nervous system can be rewired to support healing and resilience.

In therapeutic settings, the implications of the polyvagal theory are profound, particularly in trauma-informed therapy. This approach acknowledges the impact of trauma on the nervous system and emphasizes the importance of creating a safe and supportive environment for healing. By understanding the polyvagal processes, therapists can guide clients in recognizing their physiological responses and developing strategies to activate the social engagement circuit. This activation can reduce the grip of immobilization and mobilization states, fostering a sense of safety and connection. Techniques such as deep breathing, vocal exercises, and gentle movement can stimulate the vagus nerve, aiding the transition from defensive to social states. These practices empower individuals to reclaim their sense of agency and enhance their capacity for self-regulation, supporting long-term recovery and emotional well-being.

The application of polyvagal theory extends beyond therapy rooms into the fabric of our daily lives. Engaging in social interactions through conversation, shared activities, or communal experiences can stimulate the vagus nerve and activate the social engagement system. Simple acts like making eye contact, smiling, or listening attentively can foster a sense of belonging and safety, reducing stress and enhancing emotional health. These strategies for stress reduction through social interaction are accessible and effective, providing practical tools for nurturing connections and building resilience. By integrating polyvagal-informed practices into our routines, we create environments that support our nervous system's natural inclination towards safety and connection, paving the way for healthier relationships and a more balanced life.

1.6 Common Misconceptions About Vagus Nerve Functionality

Misconceptions often cloud the vagus nerve's true potential when exploring it. One frequent myth suggests that stimulating it yields instant results like flicking a switch. While some may notice immediate calming effects, achieving lasting benefits requires consistent and mindful practice. The vagus nerve is not a quick fix; it is part of a holistic approach that complements other lifestyle changes. Think of it as nurturing a garden; you wouldn't expect roses overnight, but with care and attention, they will bloom.

Another misconception revolves around vagal tone, often overestimated in its effects when isolated from lifestyle changes. A high vagal tone is beneficial but does not act in a vacuum. It reflects a well-balanced autonomic nervous system, which is influenced by factors such as physical activity, diet, and stress management. Simply focusing on vagal tone may lead to limited improvements without addressing these broader elements. It's akin to tuning just one string on a guitar and expecting the entire instrument to sound harmonious. The key lies in integrating vagal exercises with a comprehensive approach to health.

Misunderstandings also surround the principles of the polyvagal theory, particularly the concepts of "fight or flight" versus "rest and digest." Some view these states as binary, flipping from one to the other. However, the polyvagal theory introduces a more nuanced understanding. Our responses to stress are layered, involving complex interactions that include a social engagement system. This system allows us to assess safety and danger in our environment, shaping our physiological responses. Recognizing this complexity can empower individuals to foster environments that support their social engagement system, enhancing their ability to navigate stress.

When it comes to self-administered vagus nerve therapies, misconceptions can lead to misguided practices. Some assume that sporadic engagement with these techniques will suffice. However, consistency is crucial for meaningful results. Like building muscle, regular practice strengthens your vagus nerve's ability to regulate stress and promote relaxation. Whether through daily meditation, breathing exercises, or gentle yoga, incorporating these practices into your routine is pivotal. It's not about grand gestures but the small, consistent actions that accumulate over time, much like a steady stream carving a canyon.

To illustrate, consider someone introducing daily deep breathing exercises into their routine. Initially, they might feel little difference, but the practice can profoundly influence their stress levels, emotional regulation, and overall well-being over weeks and months. This is the essence of working with the vagus nerve—not through bursts of effort but consistent and deliberate engagement. By embracing this approach, individuals can dispel myths and align their practices with science, reaping the full benefits of vagus nerve stimulation.

In dispelling these myths, we open the door to understanding the vagus nerve's true potential. This nerve offers a pathway to improved mental health but requires patience, understanding, and integration with broader lifestyle changes. By clarifying these misconceptions, we empower you to engage with this work authentically and effectively. The vagus nerve is more than an anatomical curiosity; it is a dynamic participant in our health and happiness. With informed practice, you can cultivate its benefits, embracing a life of balance and resilience.

Chapter 2:

THE VAGUS NERVE AND MENTAL HEALTH

In a quiet café in the city's heart, an unassuming conversation unfolded between two friends. One of them, James, spoke candidly about his recent struggles with mood swings and persistent feelings of melancholy. He described days when getting out of bed felt like lifting a mountain. His therapist friend gently introduced him to the concept of the vagus nerve—a revelation that would soon become a turning point in James's life. This nerve, she explained, wasn't just a part of his nervous system; it was a gateway to understanding and improving his mental health. As they sipped their coffee, she shared stories of individuals whose lives had been transformed by tapping into the potential of their vagus nerve, igniting a spark of hope in James's eyes.

The vagus nerve, intricate and far-reaching, is a crucial player in our body's symphony of functions. It meanders from the brainstem, weaving through the neck and chest, and extends its influence to the abdomen. This nerve forms a vital part of the parasympathetic nervous system, known for promoting relaxation and recovery. However, its significance goes beyond physical regulation; it profoundly influences mental health by influencing mood and emotional balance. Studies have shown that vagal tone, a measure of the vagus nerve's activity, is intricately linked to mood disorders like depression. High vagal tone is associated with more excellent emotional stability and resilience, while low vagal tone often correlates with depressive symptoms. This connection has been explored in various research endeavors, highlighting the potential of vagus nerve stimulation as a therapeutic approach.

One such study, published in the Journal of Clinical Psychology, examined the relationship between vagal tone and depressive symptoms. Researchers found that individuals with higher vagal tone experienced fewer depressive episodes and reported better emotional regulation. This study underscores the importance of vagal tone as a biomarker for mental health, offering insights into how our bodies and minds are interconnected. The physiological mechanisms underlying this connection are rooted in the vagus nerve's ability to modulate neurotransmitter activity, particularly serotonin. Serotonin is the "feel-good" neurotransmitter and is crucial to mood regulation. The vagus nerve influences serotonin release, enhancing its availability and contributing to improved mood and emotional well-being.

Moreover, the vagus nerve's impact extends to inflammation, a key factor in mood disorders. Chronic inflammation has been linked to depression, and the vagus nerve plays a vital role in modulating inflammatory responses. By promoting an anti-inflammatory state, the vagus nerve helps reduce the physiological burden associated with mood disorders. This dual action of influencing neurotransmitter activity and inflammation highlights the multifaceted nature of the vagus nerve's contribution to mental health. Lifestyle choices can significantly influence vagal tone. Regular physical activity, for instance, has been shown to enhance vagal tone by promoting cardiovascular health and reducing stress. Walking, yoga, or dance activities can stimulate the vagus nerve, fostering relaxation and emotional balance. Additionally, a balanced diet rich in omega-3 fatty acids supports vagal function by reducing inflammation and promoting overall well-being.

The potential clinical applications of improving vagal tone are vast. Vagus nerve stimulation can be integrated into treatment plans for mood disorders, offering a complementary approach alongside traditional therapies. Coupled with cognitive therapy, vagal stimulation can enhance emotional regulation and resilience, providing a holistic framework for mental health care. Furthermore, wellness programs incorporating vagus nerve exercises can empower individuals to take an active role in their well-being, fostering a sense of agency and control over their mental health. The vagus nerve offers a promising avenue for enhancing mental health through accessible and effective interventions. By understanding its role in mood regulation and emotional balance, we can harness its potential to promote well-being and resilience. The journey of exploring the vagus nerve is not just about physiological insights; it's about discovering a pathway to healing and empowerment.

2.2 Anxiety and the Vagus Nerve: A Double-Edged Sword

Imagine standing on the edge of a busy street, overwhelmed by the cacophony of honking cars and bustling pedestrians. Your heart races, your breath quickens, and a familiar dread creeps in. This scene is all too common for those grappling with anxiety. With its dual role, the vagus nerve can soothe or amplify these sensations. Known for its calming effects on the heart, the vagus nerve can slow a racing pulse and encourage deep, steady breaths. Yet, when vagal tone is low, it can exacerbate anxiety, leaving you feeling trapped in a cycle of heightened arousal and distress.

Physiologically, low vagal tone can lead to a persistent state of hyperarousal. This manifests as an increased heart rate, shallow breathing, and heightened alertness. Such responses are remnants of our evolutionary past, priming the body for fight or flight. In modern life, however, these responses often arise in situations that don't warrant such intensity, like daily stressors or crowded spaces. As your body remains on high alert, anxiety symptoms can spiral, making it challenging to find calm. This is where understanding and influencing vagal tone becomes crucial. By consciously engaging the vagus nerve, you can shift the balance, promoting relaxation and reducing the grip of anxiety.

Several interventions have proven effective in moderating anxiety through vagal stimulation. For instance, progressive muscle relaxation involves tensing and slowly releasing each muscle group. This practice reduces physical tension and signals the vagus nerve to induce relaxation. Similarly, guided imagery exercises invite you to visualize peaceful scenes, engaging your senses to create a mental escape from anxiety-inducing environments. These techniques activate the parasympathetic nervous system, counteracting the stress response and fostering a sense of calm and safety.

Consider the case of Alex, a young professional who frequently experienced panic attacks during high-pressure meetings.

With guidance, Alex learned to incorporate breathwork into his routine, focusing on slow, deep breaths to engage the vagus nerve. Over time, he noticed a significant reduction in the frequency and intensity of his panic attacks. By practicing conscious breathing, Alex activated his vagus nerve, calming his heart rate and easing his anxiety. This simple yet powerful technique became a reliable tool in his arsenal against anxiety, demonstrating the practical application of vagal stimulation in managing overwhelming emotions.

The vagus nerve's role in anxiety is indeed a double-edged sword, capable of both alleviating and exacerbating symptoms. By understanding its influence and engaging in targeted practices, you can tip the scales in favor of calm and balance. Integrating these techniques into your daily life creates a foundation for resilience, helping you navigate the challenges of anxiety with greater ease. Through mindful engagement with your vagus nerve, you have the potential to transform your experience of anxiety, cultivating a sense of peace and control in life's uncertainties.

2.3 Depression: Unraveling the Vagal Connection

Throughout history, depression has been a shadow that dims the light of those it touches, casting a pall over daily life. Surprisingly, the vagus nerve—the body's natural communication network— plays a pivotal role in this shadowy landscape. Research has consistently demonstrated a correlation between low vagal tone and the frequency of depressive episodes. When the vagal tone is low, the body's ability to return to a calm state is compromised, contributing to prolonged periods of despair. This connection is not just theoretical; it has practical implications for approaching depression treatment. Vagal nerve stimulation (VNS) emerges as a beacon of hope in this context. Recognized by the FDA, VNS offers a therapeutic avenue for those battling treatment-resistant depression. By delivering mild electrical pulses to the vagus nerve, this therapy influences brain areas involved in mood regulation and has shown promising results. Long-term studies have revealed that patients receiving VNS experience significant improvements in mood and reductions in depressive symptoms. For many, VNS provides a new lease on life, offering relief where traditional treatments may have faltered.

Complementing VNS with lifestyle changes can enhance its effects and offer a holistic approach to managing depression. Mindfulness meditation, a practice rooted in ancient traditions, encourages present-moment awareness and fosters a sense of inner peace. Practicing regularly can activate the vagus nerve, promoting relaxation and emotional stability. Additionally, regular physical activity has been shown to boost vagal tone, further supporting mood stabilization. Whether it's a gentle yoga session, a brisk walk, or an invigorating dance class, movement invigorates both body and mind, laying the groundwork for recovery. Imagine a patient named Karen, who spent years entrenched in a battle against depression that seemed unyielding. Traditional treatments offered little solace, leaving her feeling adrift. Then, she was introduced to VNS, and her world shifted. Karen noticed a transformation as the gentle pulses of VNS worked in tandem with her new mindfulness practice and daily walks. The weight of depression began to lift, replaced by a newfound sense of hope. Her story illustrates the potential for VNS and lifestyle changes to create a powerful synergy, fostering healing and renewal.

Incorporating these practices into daily life can be both a challenge and a triumph. The journey requires commitment and patience, but the rewards are tangible. As individuals explore the intersection of VNS and lifestyle changes, they embark on a path toward reclaiming their emotional well-being. The vagus nerve serves as a guide, offering a roadmap to navigate the complexities of depression with resilience and grace.

2.4 Trauma Recovery:
Healing Through the Vagus Nerve

Imagine the aftermath of a storm. The skies have cleared, but the landscape remains altered. For many who have endured trauma, the internal world feels similarly changed—unpredictable and tumultuous. With its profound influence on the body's stress response system, the vagus nerve offers a pathway to recalibration. This nerve plays a pivotal role in modulating stress responses by impacting the hypothalamic-pituitary-adrenal (HPA) axis, a central player in the body's reaction to stress. Typically, the HPA axis releases hormones like cortisol to help manage stress, but in those with trauma, this system can become dysregulated, leading to chronic stress responses. By engaging the vagus nerve, you can gently guide this system back into balance, reducing the physiological hold trauma may have on your body.

Several techniques can be employed to leverage the vagus nerve for healing. Somatic experiencing exercises focus on recognizing and releasing the physical tension that trauma often encapsulates within the body. These exercises involve tuning into bodily sensations and allowing them to move through the body without judgment or resistance. For example, by simply noticing a tightness in the chest and consciously relaxing, the vagus nerve can be stimulated, signaling the body to shift toward a calm state. Grounding techniques, such as feeling the weight of your body in a chair or focusing on the sensation of your feet on the ground, can also activate the vagus nerve. These practices help anchor you in the present moment, reducing the power of traumatic memories and allowing the body to reset.

Polyvagal theory offers valuable insights into trauma therapy by emphasizing the importance of safety and connection. This theory, which explains how the nervous system responds to danger and safety cues, is increasingly integrated into trauma-informed care models. Therapists use these principles to help clients understand their physiological responses and develop strategies to engage the vagus nerve. For instance, practicing slow, deep breathing in a safe, supportive environment can activate the vagus nerve's calming pathways, promoting security. Through the lens of polyvagal theory, individuals can begin to reframe their responses to trauma, recognizing that their reactions are rooted in the body's innate survival mechanisms.

Survivors' stories often illuminate the path to recovery through vagal stimulation. Take the story of Mia, who found solace in somatic therapy after years of battling post-traumatic stress. Mia learned to tune into her body's signals through guided sessions emphasizing body awareness and gentle movement. She discovered that by engaging her vagus nerve through these practices, she could gradually diminish the grip of her traumatic memories. Over time, Mia reported feeling more grounded and less reactive to triggers, illustrating the power of vagal stimulation in facilitating trauma recovery.

As you explore these techniques, it's essential to approach them with patience and self-compassion. The process of healing from trauma is not linear, and each individual's experience is unique. By incorporating vagus nerve-focused practices into daily life, you can nurture a sense of resilience and empowerment. These techniques serve as tools to help transform the body's response to trauma, fostering a sense of safety and allowing for the emergence of inner peace.

2.5 PTSD and the Role of Vagal Stimulation

Post-traumatic stress disorder (PTSD) casts a long shadow, altering the very fabric of one's existence. At its core, PTSD represents a disruption in the autonomic nervous system, particularly a heightened state of sympathetic activity. This heightened arousal, a hallmark of PTSD, leaves individuals in a perpetual state of readiness as if danger lurks at every corner. Symptoms such as hyperarousal manifest through insomnia, irritability, and a pervasive sense of tension. Flashbacks, another common symptom, can transport individuals back to the original trauma, blurring the lines between past and present. These experiences are not merely psychological; they evoke a full-body response that reinforces the cycle of trauma.

Vagal stimulation offers a promising avenue for modulating these effects. By engaging the vagus nerve, individuals can tap into the calming influence of the parasympathetic nervous system, counterbalancing the overactivity of the sympathetic response. This modulation can significantly reduce hyperarousal symptoms, providing a respite from the constant state of alertness. Moreover, vagal stimulation has been shown to improve sleep patterns, a crucial aspect of recovery for those with PTSD. Restorative sleep offers the body a chance to heal, helping to reset the nervous system and promote emotional resilience. As the body transitions from a state of chronic stress to one of relaxation, the grip of PTSD can begin to loosen.

Clinical trials exploring vagal stimulation for PTSD have yielded promising results. In several pilot studies, participants reported a reduction in PTSD symptoms following vagal nerve stimulation. These studies highlight the therapeutic potential of integrating vagal stimulation into treatment plans. Participants experienced not only a decrease in hyperarousal but also improvements in emotional regulation and a reduction in intrusive thoughts. These findings underscore the importance of vagal stimulation as a viable complement to existing therapies, offering a new dimension of hope for those struggling with PTSD.

Integrating vagal techniques with existing therapies can amplify their efficacy. For example, exposure therapy, a standard treatment for PTSD, involves gradually confronting feared situations or memories. When combined with vagal stimulation, exposure therapy can become more manageable, as the calming effects of the vagus nerve help mitigate the anxiety associated with confronting trauma. Techniques such as deep breathing or gentle yoga, practiced before or after exposure sessions, can enhance the therapeutic process.

These practices activate the vagus nerve, reducing stress and fostering a sense of safety, crucial in trauma recovery. The integration of vagal techniques into therapeutic settings requires collaboration between practitioners and clients. By tailoring interventions to the individual's needs, therapists can create a supportive environment that encourages healing. This approach empowers individuals to actively participate in their recovery actively, fostering a sense of agency and control over their healing process.

The potential of vagal stimulation to transform the treatment landscape for PTSD is profound. It offers a pathway to healing that is both accessible and effective, providing individuals with tools to navigate the complexities of trauma. By understanding the interplay between the vagus nerve and PTSD, individuals can cultivate resilience and reclaim a sense of peace. The journey of recovery is deeply personal, but with the support of vagal stimulation, it becomes a journey filled with possibility and hope.

2.6 Emotional Regulation: Harnessing the Vagus Nerve

In the labyrinth of emotional experiences, the vagus nerve stands as a guiding thread, intricately linked to the limbic system—a network in the brain responsible for emotions and memory. This nerve communicates directly with the amygdala, the emotional epicenter that processes fear and pleasure, and the prefrontal cortex, which governs decision-making and impulse control. Together, these interactions shape our emotional responses. When the vagus nerve functions optimally, it acts as a soothing balm, modulating signals between the amygdala and prefrontal cortex. This modulation helps shift the brain from reactive states to more balanced, rational responses, enabling you to manage emotions more easily.

Certain practices prove invaluable in enhancing emotional regulation through vagal stimulation. Diaphragmatic breathing, for instance, is a simple yet profound exercise. By focusing on slow, deep breaths that engage the diaphragm, you encourage the vagus nerve to activate, promoting relaxation and emotional steadiness. This technique calms the body and signals the brain to reduce stress hormones, creating a feedback loop of calm. Similarly, body scanning techniques invite you to bring awareness to each part of your body, noticing sensations without judgment. The vagus nerve is gently stimulated as you mentally scan from head to toe, encouraging relaxation and heightened bodily awareness. These practices cultivate a mindful presence, helping you respond to emotional triggers with composure.

Over time, improved vagal tone offers long-lasting benefits for emotional health. You'll find that resilience to stress becomes natural, allowing you to navigate life's challenges confidently.

This enhanced resilience is not just about enduring stress but thriving in its presence, turning potential stressors into opportunities for growth. As the vagal tone strengthens, it fosters a robust emotional foundation, reducing the frequency and intensity of emotional outbursts. Imagine facing a tense situation and finding yourself calm and collected. Feelings that once overwhelmed you are now manageable. This shift is the hallmark of a well-regulated emotional system underpinned by the steady influence of the vagus nerve.

Consider the story of Liam, a teacher who once struggled with sudden emotional outbursts that affected his work and relationships. By incorporating vagal techniques into his routine, such as daily diaphragmatic breathing and regular body scans, he noticed significant changes. His reactions became more measured, and he was less prone to frustration and anger. Over time, his improved emotional regulation transformed his classroom and personal life, allowing him to form more profound, more meaningful connections. Liam's experience exemplifies the practical outcomes achievable through vagal stimulation, illustrating the profound impact on emotional well-being.

As we conclude this chapter, it's clear that the vagus nerve is a vital player in emotional regulation, offering a path to excellent emotional health and resilience. The practices discussed provide accessible tools to engage this nerve, promoting a balanced emotional state. In the next chapter, we will explore practical exercises that further harness the vagus nerve, illuminating how these simple yet effective techniques can enhance mental and physical health.

Chapter 3:

PRACTICAL SOMATIC EXERCISES FOR VAGUS NERVE STIMULATION

In a serene park beneath a canopy of rustling leaves, a young woman named Anna was captivated by the simple act of breathing. Years of battling anxiety had left her feeling disconnected from her own body, but as she sat on a weathered bench, she discovered something transformative. Guided by her breath's gentle rise and fall, Anna sensed a newfound calm washing over her. This was not just any breathing; it was diaphragmatic breathing, a practice that would soon become her anchor in navigating life's storms. As she inhaled deeply, allowing her diaphragm to expand fully, she could almost feel the soothing touch of the vagus nerve, activating her body's innate relaxation response.

Diaphragmatic breathing, often called belly breathing, is a powerful technique that engages the diaphragm, a dome-shaped muscle beneath your lungs. By drawing air deeply into your lungs and allowing your belly to rise, you activate the parasympathetic nervous system, which governs your body's rest and digestion functions. This practice facilitates a profound sense of relaxation and strengthens the diaphragm, enhancing your overall respiratory capacity. To begin, find a comfortable position, lying on your back if possible, and place one hand on your stomach and the other on your chest. Breathe in slowly through your nose, feeling your belly rise as the diaphragm contracts, then exhale gently through your mouth, allowing the belly to fall. Regular practice, even for just 10 minutes a day, can yield remarkable benefits, calming your mind and body during stressful moments.

Another breathwork technique worth exploring is alternate nostril breathing, a practice rooted in ancient traditions that offers a unique pathway to tranquility. By balancing the airflow through both nostrils, this exercise harmonizes your brain's left and right hemispheres, promoting a state of equilibrium and peace. Sit comfortably with your spine straight, close your right nostril with your thumb, and inhale deeply through your left nostril. Then, close your left nostril with your ring finger, release your right nostril, and exhale through it. Reverse the process, inhaling through the right nostril and exhaling through the left.

This rhythmic alternation can be repeated for several minutes, ideally in the morning or before bed, to set a serene tone for your day or to ease into restful sleep.

Physiologically, breathwork exercises like these impact the vagus nerve by increasing heart rate variability (HRV), a key indicator of autonomic nervous system health. A higher HRV signifies a more adaptable and resilient nervous system capable of effectively managing stress and maintaining balance. Through intentional breathing, you stimulate the vagus nerve, which moderates your heart rate and promotes relaxation. This cascading effect helps lower blood pressure, reduce cortisol levels, and enhance emotional regulation—an invaluable asset in managing anxiety and depression.

Breathwork can be tailored to address specific situations with remarkable efficacy. You might find solace in a quick breathing exercise such as the 4-7-8 technique in acute stress. Inhale quietly through your nose for a count of four, hold your breath for seven, and exhale completely through your mouth for a count of eight. This technique, practiced several times, can swiftly calm your nervous system, providing a portable sanctuary of peace amid chaos. Whether you're facing a hectic day at work or a sleepless night, these breathwork practices serve as accessible tools to center yourself and engage the healing potential of your vagus nerve, guiding you toward a state of calm and resilience.

Interactive Exercise: Journaling Your Breathwork Experience

Take a moment to reflect on your breathwork practice. Consider how your body and mind feel before and after engaging in diaphragmatic or alternate nostril breathing. Use a journal to note any changes in your mood, physical sensations, or thoughts. Record the duration of your practice and any insights you gain. Reflect on how these exercises influence your day-to-day stress levels and emotional well-being. This reflective practice can enhance your awareness and deepen your connection to the healing power of your breath.

3.1 Meditation Practices to Stimulate the Vagus Nerve

Meditation is key to unlocking a calmer, more regulated emotional state by directly influencing vagal tone. By engaging in meditation, you can enhance your ability to manage stress and emotions. Cultivating mindfulness and awareness through meditation allows you to observe your thoughts and feelings without being overwhelmed. This practice nurtures a space of inner peace, where the sympathetic nervous system takes a backseat, and the parasympathetic system, orchestrated by the vagus nerve, comes to the fore. As you settle into meditation, you invite your body to relax, your heart rate to slow, and your mind to find clarity.

Loving-kindness meditation, also known as "metta" meditation, is a practice that encourages you to direct warmth and compassion toward yourself and others. This form of meditation strengthens the bonds of empathy and self-kindness, crucial elements for emotional well-being. To begin, find a comfortable seated position, and with each inhale, silently repeat phrases of goodwill such as "May I be happy" or "May I be safe." Gradually extend these sentiments to friends, family, and eventually even those you find challenging. This practice opens your heart to compassion and stimulates the vagus nerve, encouraging a state of calm and connection. Regular engagement with loving-kindness meditation can increase empathy and reduce negative emotions, fostering a more harmonious relationship with yourself and the world.

On the other hand, focused attention meditation is about honing your concentration on a single point of focus, such as your breath, a mantra, or a candle flame. This practice strengthens the mind-body connection by training you to redirect your attention whenever it wanders gently. It is a mental exercise that, over time, enhances your ability to remain present and centered. To practice, choose a focus and settle into a quiet space. As distractions arise, acknowledge them without judgment and gently bring your attention back to your chosen focus point. This repeated redirection sharpens your concentration and activates the vagus nerve, promoting stability and calm. Through focused attention meditation, you develop a resilient mind less swayed by external chaos, allowing for greater emotional regulation.

Scientific research supports meditation's effectiveness in enhancing vagal tone and well-being. Studies have shown that regular meditation practice is linked to improved emotional regulation, reduced anxiety, and increased resilience. For instance, research published in "Psychosomatic Medicine" indicates that meditation can positively influence heart rate variability, a marker of vagal tone, suggesting a healthier autonomic nervous system. By engaging in meditation, you nurture your mental health and strengthen the physiological foundation that supports it. This blend of science and practice highlights meditation's role in promoting a balanced and peaceful life.

With its diverse practices, meditation offers a versatile toolkit for enhancing vagal tone and emotional well-being. Whether you're drawn to the compassion of loving-kindness or the discipline of focused attention, these practices provide accessible pathways to greater calm and resilience. In the quietude of meditation, the vagus nerve finds its ally, guiding you toward a more centered and harmonious existence.

3.2 Gentle Yoga: Poses for Vagal Activation

In the serene space of your living room or a quiet corner of a park, yoga unfolds as more than just a series of poses; it becomes a gateway to inner calm and balance. The Cat-Cow stretch is a gentle yet powerful way to engage your spine and stimulate the vagus nerve among the myriad poses. As you position yourself on all fours, align your wrists under your shoulders and knees under your hips. For the Cat pose, exhale as you arch your back, tucking your chin to your chest, and draw your belly button to your spine. Transition smoothly into the Cow pose by inhaling deeply, allowing your belly to drop as you lift your chest and gaze gently upward. This fluid motion enhances spinal flexibility and synchronizes breath and movement, weaving a tapestry of relaxation through your nervous system.

Equally calming is the Legs-up-the-wall pose, a sanctuary for both body and mind. Find a wall, sit sideways next to it, and gently swing your legs up while reclining your back on the ground. Allow your arms to rest lightly at your sides, palms facing upward. This inversion promotes circulation and invites the parasympathetic nervous system to take over, fostering a deep sense of relaxation and stress relief. Your breath steadies as your legs rest against the wall, and your mind finds respite from the day's demands. Regular practice of this pose can ease tension, reduce anxiety, and create a cocoon of tranquility within your busy life.

Yoga is not merely about the poses; it's about the dance of breath and movement. Each transition in yoga is an opportunity to connect deeply with your breath, creating a seamless flow that engages the vagus nerve. As you breathe in harmony with each movement, you harness the power of breath to amplify the calming effects of yoga. This coordination not only magnifies the benefits of each pose but also cultivates a meditative state, where stress dissipates and serenity prevails. In this union of breath and movement, you nurture a holistic practice that extends beyond the mat, infusing your daily life with balance and peace.

The transformative impact of yoga on the nervous system is profound, particularly in its ability to reduce stress and anxiety. When practiced regularly, yoga becomes a tool for decreasing cortisol levels, the hormone associated with stress. This reduction fosters a more stable emotional state and bolsters resilience against life's challenges. Through gentle yoga, the body learns to unwind, the mind finds clarity, and the heart beats calmly. As stress ebbs away, the nervous system recalibrates, paving the way for emotional well-being and mental clarity.

For those new to yoga, a beginner-friendly sequence like the Sun Salutation offers a comprehensive introduction. With modifications for all skill levels, this sequence guides you through a flowing series of poses that invigorate the body and calm the mind. Begin in Mountain pose, standing tall, and transition into a Forward Fold, allowing your body to hang loosely. Continue into Plank pose, lowering gracefully into Cobra, then press back into Downward-Facing Dog. As you move through each pose, focus on the rhythm of your breath, allowing it to guide you with ease and intention. This sequence practiced regularly, becomes a cornerstone for developing strength, flexibility, and serenity.

With its gentle poses and mindful breathing, yoga becomes an ally in nurturing the vagus nerve and fostering emotional resilience. It invites you to explore your body with curiosity and kindness, transforming each pose into a sanctuary of calm. As you embrace the practice of yoga, you cultivate a deeper connection with yourself, promoting a sense of peace that extends beyond the mat.

3.3 Mindful Movement: Integrating Body and Mind

The mindful movement is a refreshing contrast to traditional exercise, where the focus is often on intensity and physical exertion. In mindful movement, the spotlight shifts to awareness and presence during each action. It is not about how fast you move or how many repetitions you complete but rather about the quality of your attention and connection to your body. This practice invites you to slow down and tune in to your bodily sensations, aligning your mind and body in a harmonious dance. Mindful movement encourages you to notice the subtle shifts in your muscles, the rhythm of your breath, and the grounding sensation of your feet touching the earth. This awareness fosters a deeper connection to yourself, allowing you to experience movement as a form of meditation in motion.

Tai Chi and Qigong exemplify mindful movement principles, embodying the art of slow, deliberate actions that enhance balance and vagal tone. These ancient practices, often described as moving meditations, cultivate a sense of calm through their gentle, flowing sequences. In Tai Chi, each movement is purposeful, encouraging you to engage with your breathing and maintain an attentive presence. As you shift your weight from one foot to the other, you enhance your balance, stimulating the vagus nerve and promoting relaxation. Similarly, Qigong involves a series of postures and breathing techniques that harmonize energy flow within the body. This practice strengthens your physical resilience and nurtures inner tranquility, reducing stress and enhancing overall well-being. Integrating Tai Chi and Qigong into your routine invites a soothing rhythm into your life, transforming movement into a sanctuary of peace.

Mindfulness can be woven into the fabric of your everyday activities, inviting you to bring a meditative quality to the mundane. Consider the simple act of walking. Mindful walking encourages you to savor each step instead of rushing from one destination to another. Feel the texture of the ground beneath your feet, notice the gentle sway of your arms, and immerse yourself in the sights and sounds around you. This practice transforms walking into a sensory experience, grounding you in the present moment and activating the vagus nerve. Similarly, conscious stretching invites you to explore your body's range of motion with curiosity and care. As you stretch, focus on the sensations in your muscles, the lengthening and release, and the space you create within your body. These everyday activities become opportunities to cultivate mindfulness, offering moments of tranquility amidst the chaos of daily life.

Integrating mindful movement into stress management strategies provides practical applications that can be seamlessly incorporated into your routine. Consider taking mindful movement breaks during work hours, especially when stress mounts. Stand up from your desk, stretch gently, and take a few conscious breaths. Pay attention to how your body feels as you move, releasing tension with each exhale. These brief interludes invigorate your body and refresh your mind, enhancing focus and productivity. By incorporating mindful movement into your day, you create pockets of peace that counteract stress, fostering a more balanced and centered existence. Whether through Tai Chi, mindful walking, or a simple stretch, these practices offer a gentle yet powerful means to engage with your body and mind, nurturing a calm and connection that supports your overall well-being.

3.4 Sound Healing:
The Vagus Nerve and Vibrational Therapy

Sound healing offers a fascinating intersection between ancient wisdom and modern therapeutic practices, leveraging the power of sound frequencies to elicit profound effects on the vagus nerve. Sound healing operates on the principle that vibrations can influence the body's energy fields, creating a resonant environment that encourages healing and balance. With its expansive reach throughout the body, the vagus nerve responds favorably to these vibrations, which can be likened to a gentle, sonic massage for your nervous system. When sound waves interact with your body, they stimulate the vagus nerve, promoting relaxation and reducing stress. This interaction is not just about the pleasant sounds you hear; it's about the vibrational energy that permeates your being, coaxing the vagus nerve into action and fostering a state of tranquility.

Tools such as singing bowls and tuning forks are frequently employed in therapeutic settings to harness these healing vibrations. Traditionally crafted from metal or crystal, singing bowls produce rich, harmonic tones when struck or circled with a mallet. As the bowl sings, its vibrations resonate through the air and your body, creating a soundscape that invites the vagus nerve to engage its calming powers. During meditation, placing a singing bowl on your body while it hums can amplify this effect, as the vibrations are directly transmitted to your tissues and nerves. Tuning forks, on the other hand, offer a more targeted approach. When struck, they emit a pitch that can be applied to acupressure points, channels known for their connection to the nervous system. These points serve as conduits, allowing the vibrational energy to travel along the meridians and reach the vagus nerve, facilitating a deep sense of relaxation and balance.

Vocal toning and humming provide an accessible entry into sound healing, requiring no special equipment or training. Simply using your voice to produce sound can remarkably impact the vagus nerve. The vibrations generated by humming or chanting travel through the skull and nasal passages, directly stimulating the nerve. This practice is not only simple but also profoundly effective. By experimenting with different tones and pitches, you can find the resonance that feels most soothing to your body. Engage in vocal toning exercises by humming a single note and focusing on the sensation of vibration in your chest and throat. This gentle practice can be incorporated into your daily routine as a quick reset during stressful moments or a calming ritual before sleep.

Consider the story of Mark, a man who found solace in sound healing after years of battling chronic stress. Introduced to the practice by a friend, Mark began attending weekly group sessions where singing bowls and tuning forks were used. He noticed an immediate difference, describing the sessions as a release from the constant tension that plagued him. Inspired by his experiences, Mark started incorporating vocal toning into his daily routine. Each morning, he would spend a few minutes humming softly, feeling the vibrations resonate through his body. Over time, Mark reported a noticeable reduction in his stress levels and an increased sense of calm. His journey highlights the transformative potential of sound therapy, illustrating how these practices can be woven into everyday life to enhance well-being.

Sound healing is a testament to the body's innate ability to heal through resonance and vibration. By engaging in these practices, you can tap into a source of calm and balance, nurturing the vagus nerve and enhancing your overall mental and physical health.

3.5 Cold Exposure:
A Surprising Ally for Vagal Stimulation

Cold exposure might seem counterintuitive when seeking comfort, yet it has emerged as a powerful tool for enhancing vagal tone and promoting overall well-being. You trigger a fascinating physiological response when you expose your body to cold, such as through a brisk shower or a splash of icy water on your face. The initial shiver and gasp signal the activation of the parasympathetic nervous system, mediated by the vagus nerve. This activation counterbalances the body's initial stress response, helping to calm the mind and stabilize emotions. The cold acts as a catalyst, inviting your body to adapt and embrace a state of relaxation, even in the face of discomfort.

Incorporating cold exposure into your routine can be both invigorating and revitalizing. Starting with cold showers is a practical and accessible method. Begin by finishing your regular warm shower with a brief burst of cold water, gradually extending the duration as your tolerance builds. Allow the cold water to cascade over your body, focusing on steady, controlled breathing. This practice invigorates your body and strengthens your resilience to stress. Using cold packs on the face or neck can be effective for a more targeted approach. Applying a cold pack to these areas can stimulate the vagus nerve directly, providing a refreshing reset to your nervous system whenever you need a quick pick-me-up.

The benefits of cold exposure on mental health have garnered significant attention in recent years. Scientific studies have shown that regular cold exposure can lead to a reduction in symptoms of anxiety and depression. The physiological response to cold involves the release of endorphins and an increase in norepinephrine levels, which contribute to improved mood and enhanced emotional resilience. By incorporating cold exposure into your life, you tap into a natural and empowering way to bolster your mental health, fostering a sense of vitality and alertness that can carry you through the day's challenges.

While the idea of cold exposure may initially feel daunting, it's essential to approach it with mindfulness and care. Start with brief exposures, allowing your body to acclimate to the sensation. Gradually increase the duration and intensity as your comfort grows. Always listen to your body's signals, and never push beyond your limits. The goal is to safely embrace the benefits of cold exposure, ensuring your experience is both positive and sustainable. With patience and practice, cold exposure can become a cornerstone of your wellness routine, offering a refreshing counterpoint to the stresses of modern life.

As we wrap up this chapter, it's clear that the vagus nerve can be engaged through various accessible and effective practices, from breathwork and meditation to yoga, mindful movement, and sound healing. Each technique offers unique benefits, providing enhanced emotional regulation and resilience pathways. Cold exposure adds a dynamic element to these practices, expanding your toolkit for nurturing mental well-being. As you explore these methods, you'll discover that the vagus nerve is not just a physiological entity but a bridge to greater harmony between mind and body. Moving forward, we'll integrate these practices with other therapeutic modalities, unlocking further potential for growth and healing.

Chapter 4:

INTEGRATING VAGUS NERVE TECHNIQUES WITH OTHER THERAPIES

Imagine sitting across from your therapist, an unspoken weight hanging between you. You've been here before, delving into the depths of your mind with Cognitive Behavioral Therapy (CBT), yet something always seems amiss. Today, however, your therapist suggests a new approach. She invites you to take a deep breath, drawing it slowly into your lungs, and as you do, she explains the connection between the breath and the vagus nerve—a link that could transform your therapy experience. This simple act of breathing, engaging your body alongside your mind, becomes the bridge between the cerebral and the somatic, between thought and feeling. In this chapter, we explore how the integration of vagal stimulation with CBT can enhance the effectiveness of both, offering a holistic approach to healing trauma, anxiety, and depression.

Cognitive Behavioral Therapy is a well-established method that identifies and challenges negative thought patterns to alter behavioral responses. By integrating vagal stimulation into CBT, we open the door to a more comprehensive therapeutic experience. The synergy between these two approaches lies in their complementary nature. While CBT addresses cognitive distortions and helps restructure thought patterns, vagal stimulation calms the nervous system. This integration allows you to simultaneously tackle emotional and physiological responses, creating a more balanced and effective therapy. For instance, as you engage in cognitive restructuring, the calming effects of vagal exercises, such as deep breathing, can reduce the physiological stress responses often accompanying challenging mental work. This dual approach enhances emotional regulation, reinforcing positive thought patterns and facilitating lasting change.

During CBT sessions, the vagus nerve activation can significantly reduce physiological stress responses. Many individuals experience somatic symptoms, such as increased heart rate or muscle tension, during exposure therapy—a standard component of CBT for anxiety and trauma-related disorders. These symptoms can be alleviated by incorporating vagal stimulation techniques, providing a more comfortable and manageable experience. Deep breathing exercises, for example, can be used before engaging in cognitive exercises, helping to ground you and prepare your body and mind for the work ahead. This integration enhances CBT's effectiveness and promotes a sense of safety and stability, which is crucial for navigating the complexities of exposure therapy.

Practical strategies for clinicians seeking to incorporate vagal techniques into CBT sessions are both accessible and valuable. Encouraging clients to engage in deep breathing exercises at the start of each session can set a calming tone and help regulate the autonomic nervous system. As clients progress through cognitive exercises, reminders to periodically return to the breath can anchor them in the present moment, reducing anxiety and enhancing focus. Clinicians might also incorporate guided imagery or mindfulness exercises, stimulating the vagus nerve and supporting cognitive work. These practices enrich the therapeutic experience and empower clients to develop self-regulation skills they can use outside of therapy.

Consider the story of a therapist named Dr. Mason, who began integrating vagal techniques into her CBT practice. She recounts the case of Tom, a client who struggled with panic attacks and found traditional CBT overwhelming at times. Dr. Mason witnessed a transformation by introducing deep breathing and gentle yoga poses into their sessions. Tom reported feeling more centered and less reactive to triggers, allowing him to engage more fully in cognitive exercises. Over time, his panic attacks decreased in frequency and intensity, and he expressed a newfound sense of control over his emotional responses. Dr. Mason's integration of vagal techniques not only enhanced the therapeutic outcomes for Tom but also deepened their therapeutic relationship, fostering trust and collaboration.

The potential for growth and healing is immense for those seeking to integrate these approaches into their lives or practices. By combining the cognitive insights of CBT with the physiological benefits of vagal stimulation, you create a holistic framework for addressing trauma, anxiety, and depression. This integration offers a comprehensive pathway to healing, where mind and body work in harmony to support your journey toward well-being. Through this collaborative approach, you can access a deeper understanding of yourself and cultivate the resilience to navigate life's challenges with grace and strength.

Case Study Reflection: Integrating Vagal Techniques in Therapy

Reflect on a therapy session where vagal techniques were integrated. Consider the changes you observed in your emotional and physiological responses. How did incorporating breathing or movement exercises impact your ability to engage with cognitive work? Use this reflection to explore how these practices might be further integrated into your healing journey, enhancing your emotional regulation and overall well-being.

4.1 Mindfulness-Based Stress Reduction and the Vagus Nerve

Picture yourself sitting quietly, focusing on the gentle rhythm of your breath. The world's distractions fade as you anchor yourself in the present moment—this practice, known as Mindfulness-Based Stress Reduction (MBSR), centers on cultivating awareness and relaxation. MBSR teaches you to engage with the here and now, promoting greater calm and clarity. By honing in on the present, you learn to observe your thoughts and feelings without judgment, allowing them to pass like clouds in a vast sky. This approach enhances your mental well-being and creates a profound connection with your body.

The significance of MBSR extends beyond mere relaxation. It is vital in enhancing vagal tone, managing stress, and regulating emotions. Mindfulness practices activate the parasympathetic nervous system, reducing chronic stress and fostering emotional equilibrium. Focusing on your breath or bodily sensations stimulates the vagus nerve, lowering the heart rate and promoting relaxation. Reducing stress responses improves mental health as the body learns to shift more readily from fight-or-flight states to restorative modes.

Exercises like body scan meditation should be considered to effectively integrate MBSR into your routine. This practice invites you to systematically focus on each body part, noticing sensations without judgment. By doing so, you cultivate awareness and relaxation, engaging the vagus nerve. Begin by lying down in a comfortable position, and slowly direct your attention to your feet. Gradually move your awareness upward through your legs, torso, arms, and head, observing any tension or ease. This mindful exploration relaxes your body and enhances your connection to the present moment. Guided breathing exercises further support this process. Choose a quiet space, sit comfortably, and close your eyes. Inhale deeply through your nose, allowing your belly to expand, and exhale slowly through your mouth. Focus on the sensation of breath entering and leaving your body, anchoring you in the now.

The effectiveness of MBSR in improving mental health is supported by research and personal testimonials. Studies have consistently shown that mindfulness practices can reduce symptoms of anxiety and depression. For example, a study published in the journal "Psychological Science" found that participants in an MBSR program experienced significant stress reductions and improved emotional regulation. These findings highlight the transformative potential of mindfulness in promoting well-being. Personal stories further illustrate this impact. Consider the account of a woman who struggled with chronic anxiety. Through regular engagement with MBSR, she found herself more composed and less reactive to stressors. The practice became a sanctuary, allowing her to navigate life's challenges with greater ease and resilience.

Incorporating MBSR into your life means embracing a practice supporting mental and physical health. By anchoring yourself in the present, you engage the vagus nerve and foster balance and tranquility. The benefits extend beyond the moments of practice, permeating daily life calmly and clearly. As you continue to explore the potential of MBSR, your capacity for resilience and emotional regulation grows, transforming how you experience the world around you.

4.2 Integrating Somatic Experiencing Techniques

In a world that often prioritizes mental analysis over bodily awareness, somatic experiencing emerges as a profound method for trauma healing. This approach focuses on the body's innate ability to process and release trauma through heightened awareness of bodily sensations rather than solely relying on verbal recounting of traumatic events, somatic experiencing encourages you to tune into the physical manifestations of trauma that may reside within your body. Doing so provides a pathway to release these deeply embedded tensions and restore balance. Techniques such as pendulation, a method that involves gently shifting attention between areas of tension and areas of ease within the body, are central to this practice. This oscillation helps discharge the energy trapped by trauma, promoting a return to equilibrium.

The synergy between somatic experience and vagal stimulation offers a remarkable enhancement of therapeutic outcomes. These approaches target trauma's physiological and emotional dimensions, holistically engaging the nervous system. Vagal stimulation, known for calming the autonomic nervous system, complements the somatic focus on bodily sensations, providing a dual approach to regulating stress responses. As you engage in somatic experiencing, activating the vagus nerve aids in soothing the body's fight-or-flight responses, fostering relaxation and safety. This integration not only facilitates the release of trauma but also strengthens your capacity for resilience, bridging the gap between mind and body.

Practical examples of somatic experiencing techniques demonstrate how these methods can be applied in real life. Consider pendulation exercises, where you are guided to focus on a specific area of tension, such as a tightened chest or clenched jaw. By consciously shifting your attention to a more relaxed area, like your feet or hands, and then back to the tension, you create a gentle rhythm that encourages the release of trapped energy. This practice can be done alone or with a therapist, providing a powerful tool for managing trauma responses and cultivating a sense of safety within your own body. Another effective technique involves grounding exercises engaging with your surroundings through sensory awareness, such as noticing a chair's texture or the air's temperature. These practices ground you in the present moment and stimulate the vagus nerve, promoting a sense of calm and connection.

Consider the story of Maria, a client who had long been haunted by childhood trauma. Traditional talk therapy had brought some relief, but the physical manifestations of her trauma persisted. It wasn't until she began working with a therapist trained in somatic experiencing that she experienced a shift. Through pendulation and grounding exercises, Maria learned to listen to her body's signals, gradually releasing the tension stored for years. Integrating vagal stimulation techniques, such as deep breathing during sessions, further enhanced her progress. Over time, Maria noticed reduced anxiety, improved sleep, and a newfound sense of empowerment. Her journey illustrates the profound impact of combining somatic experiencing with vagal techniques, offering hope and healing through the body's wisdom.

For those exploring these approaches, it's essential to approach them with patience and openness. Somatic experiencing invites you to trust your body's ability to heal and transform, one sensation at a time. By integrating these practices into your life, you can access a deeper level of healing, fostering resilience and well-being. This work isn't about erasing the past but learning to live alongside it with greater ease and harmony. The body holds stories, and through somatic experiencing and vagal stimulation, you can learn to listen, release, and move forward with a renewed sense of peace.

4.3 Biofeedback: Monitoring and Enhancing Vagal Response

Biofeedback is a captivating tool that bridges the gap between your body's physiological responses and conscious awareness. By providing real-time data on bodily functions, biofeedback allows you to observe and learn to control typically involuntary processes. One of the most effective biofeedback markers is heart rate variability (HRV), which measures the variation in time between each heartbeat. HRV reflects the dynamic interplay between the sympathetic and parasympathetic branches of your autonomic nervous system, with higher variability indicating a healthier and more adaptable system. When you use biofeedback to monitor HRV, you gain insight into your body's stress responses and vagal tone. This heightened awareness can empower you to manage your stress levels proactively, ultimately enhancing your mental and physical well-being.

To begin using biofeedback for vagal stimulation, you'll need a heart rate monitor capable of tracking HRV. Set up your session in a quiet, comfortable space where you won't be disturbed.

Attach the monitor according to its instructions, ensuring a snug yet comfy fit. Once you're ready, take slow, deep breaths, inhaling through your nose and exhaling through your mouth. As you breathe, observe the data displayed by the monitor. It may show a graph or series of numbers representing your HRV. The goal is to increase the variability by maintaining calm, steady breathing. This practice engages your vagus nerve and teaches you how your actions can influence your physiological state. Regular sessions can help you develop a keen sense of self-regulation, allowing you to manage stress more effectively in everyday situations.

Interpreting biofeedback data requires patience and practice. The numbers might seem abstract initially, but you'll learn to recognize patterns and understand what affects your HRV over time. For instance, you might notice a drop in variability during stress or a rise when relaxed. Use this information to identify triggers and develop strategies to enhance your vagal tone. Techniques like diaphragmatic breathing, meditation, or mindful movement can be integrated into your routine to improve your HRV. As you become more attuned to your body's signals, you'll find yourself better equipped to navigate stress, using the feedback as a guide to maintain balance and well-being.

The benefits of biofeedback extend beyond immediate stress reduction, offering a pathway to improved mental health and emotional resilience. Enhancing your self-regulating ability allows you to cultivate a sense of agency and control over your emotional responses. This newfound capacity can significantly reduce anxiety and stress, leading to a more balanced and fulfilling life. Biofeedback empowers you to engage with your body's natural rhythms, fostering a deeper connection between mind and body. This integration supports emotional regulation and cognitive function, enhancing your overall well-being.

Consider the experience of a man named Eric, who turned to biofeedback after years of struggling with anxiety. He began incorporating biofeedback sessions into his weekly routine, using the data to guide his breathing exercises. Over time, Eric noticed a marked improvement in his ability to manage stress, feeling more grounded and less reactive to daily pressures. The feedback became a tool for self-discovery, helping him identify patterns and develop healthier responses. Today, Eric credits biofeedback with transforming his approach to mental health, illustrating the profound impact this practice can have on emotional regulation and resilience.

Through biofeedback, you gain a window into your body's inner workings, learning to influence processes once thought beyond reach. By embracing this technology, you can enhance your vagal tone, fostering a state of calm and balance that supports your mental and physical health. This practice, rooted in awareness and control, offers a powerful means to engage with your body's natural rhythms, providing a foundation for lasting well-being.

4.4 Nutritional Support for Vagal Health

Imagine nutrition as a powerful ally in the quest for mental and physical well-being, mainly when supporting your vagus nerve. The foods you consume can profoundly impact your vagal tone and, by extension, your mental health. At the heart of this connection lies the intricate relationship between diet and physiology, where nutrients play a pivotal role in nerve health. Omega-3 fatty acids, for example, are crucial for maintaining the structural integrity of nerve cells and promoting their optimal function. Found abundantly in foods like salmon, flaxseeds, and walnuts, these essential fats support nerve health and have anti-inflammatory properties that can enhance mental clarity and emotional balance. Incorporating omega-3-rich foods into your diet nurtures your nervous system and promotes a resilient mental state.

To support vagal function effectively, consider embracing a diet rich in anti-inflammatory foods. Ingredients such as turmeric and ginger are renowned for reducing inflammation and easing stress on the nervous system. These spices can be easily added to meals, infusing them with flavor and health benefits. Additionally, focusing on gut-friendly foods is paramount for overall well-being. The gut-brain axis, a complex communication network, underscores the importance of gut health in mental function. By consuming probiotic-rich foods like yogurt, kefir, and sauerkraut, you enhance your gut microbiome, which in turn supports vagal health and emotional regulation. A well-nourished gut can foster a balanced mental state, highlighting the interconnectedness of diet and emotion.

The role of gut health in supporting vagal function cannot be underestimated. The gut-brain axis facilitates communication between the gut and the brain, with the vagus nerve serving as a conduit for this dialogue. A healthy gut microbiome, populated by diverse and beneficial bacteria, modulates this interaction. Probiotic-rich foods bolster the gut's ecosystem, enhancing digestion and the body's resilience to stress. This symbiotic relationship between gut health and vagal tone illustrates diet's profound impact on mental well-being. By prioritizing foods that support gut health, you are laying the groundwork for a more balanced and harmonious mental state.

Consider a sample meal plan focused on vagus-supportive ingredients for those seeking practical ways to integrate these dietary principles into daily life. Begin your day with a breakfast of Greek yogurt topped with flaxseeds and a drizzle of honey. A salad featuring mixed greens, cherry tomatoes, avocado, and grilled salmon provides a nourishing blend of omega-3s and healthy fats for lunch. A turmeric and ginger-infused lentil soup makes for a comforting and anti-inflammatory dinner. Enjoy snacks like roasted chickpeas or a handful of walnuts throughout the day, offering both satiety and nutritional benefits. This meal plan satisfies your taste buds and nourishes your nervous system, supporting your journey toward enhanced mental health and resilience.

Recipe Spotlight: Turmeric and Ginger Lentil Soup

Ingredients:

- 1 cup red lentils, rinsed
- 1 tablespoon olive oil
- 1 onion, diced
- 2 cloves garlic, minced
- 1 tablespoon fresh ginger, grated
- 1 teaspoon turmeric powder
- 1 teaspoon cumin
- 4 cups vegetable broth
- Salt and pepper to taste
- Lemon wedges for serving

Instructions:

1. Heat olive oil in a large pot over medium heat. Add onion and garlic, sautéing until translucent.

2. Stir in ginger, turmeric, and cumin, cooking for an additional minute until fragrant.

3. Add lentils and vegetable broth, bringing the mixture to a boil. Reduce heat and simmer for 20 minutes or until lentils are tender.

4. Season with salt and pepper. Serve with a squeeze of fresh lemon juice.

This simple yet nourishing soup is a testament to how nutrition can support your vagal health and overall well-being.

4.5 Sleep Hygiene: Restorative Practices for Vagal Tone

In the quiet lull between waking and dreaming, your body enters a realm of restoration and repair, a nightly ritual essential for maintaining physical and mental health. Sleep hygiene, the practice of habits that promote a good night's sleep, is crucial in supporting vagal tone. Quality sleep is a balm for the nervous system, allowing the vagus nerve to function optimally. When you sleep well, your body engages in processes that regulate stress responses and bolster emotional resilience. During these restful hours, the brain processes the day's emotions, consolidating memories and restoring balance. This restorative process is vital for emotional regulation, offering a buffer against the pressures of daily life. Adequate sleep rejuvenates the body and enhances cognitive function, mood, and overall well-being, creating a harmonious foundation for mental health.

Creating an environment conducive to sleep begins with establishing a consistent sleep schedule. Going to bed and waking up simultaneously each day helps regulate your body's internal clock, making it easier to fall asleep and wake up refreshed. Consider the bedroom as a sanctuary, a space dedicated to rest. Keep the room calm, quiet, and dark, minimizing noise and light that could disrupt sleep. Investing in a comfortable mattress and pillows can also make a significant difference. Limit exposure to screens before bed, as the blue light emitted can interfere with melatonin production, the hormone responsible for sleep regulation. Instead, develop a calming bedtime routine, such as reading a book or practicing gentle stretching, to signal your body that it's time to unwind.

The benefits of good sleep hygiene extend beyond just feeling rested. When you achieve restorative sleep, you support the vagus nerve functions, enhancing emotional regulation and stress resilience. A well-rested mind is better equipped to handle the ups and downs of life, leading to improved mood and cognitive performance. Sleep and well-being are interconnected, as adequate rest provides the mental clarity for effective decision-making and problem-solving. Studies have shown that individuals who prioritize sleep experience fewer symptoms of anxiety and depression. By nurturing your sleep habits, you create a ripple effect that positively impacts your overall health, fostering a sense of balance and vitality.

Consider the story of Lily, a reader who struggled with persistent stress and anxiety. Despite trying various relaxation techniques, she found herself perpetually exhausted. It wasn't until she prioritized her sleep hygiene that she noticed a significant shift. By establishing a consistent bedtime routine and creating a serene sleep environment, Lily experienced a newfound energy and emotional stability. Improving her sleep practices enhanced her well-being, illustrating the transformative power of quality rest. Her experience serves as a testament to the impact of sleep on mental health, highlighting how small changes can lead to profound improvements.

As we wrap up this chapter, remember that integrating these restorative practices into your life can significantly enhance your vagal tone and overall well-being. The journey to better mental health is multifaceted, and sleep is a cornerstone. By prioritizing sleep hygiene, you support your body's natural rhythms, paving the way for a more balanced and resilient life. This chapter concludes our exploration of integrated approaches to vagal health, setting the stage for further insights into mental and physical well-being.

Chapter 5:

OVERCOMING COMMON CHALLENGES IN VAGUS NERVE THERAPY

The world of vagus nerve therapy is like an unfolding story, rich with promise and potential, yet sometimes clouded by skepticism and misunderstanding. Picture a curious traveler embarking on a journey through an unfamiliar landscape, hesitant yet hopeful about what lies ahead. This chapter aims to illuminate the path, dispelling doubts and clarifying the science behind vagus nerve therapy, especially for those seeking solace from trauma, anxiety, and depression. By breaking down complex concepts into digestible insights, we aim to build a bridge between scientific understanding and personal healing, empowering you to navigate this therapeutic terrain confidently.

Understanding the vagus nerve's influence on emotional regulation is crucial to appreciating its therapeutic potential. This nerve acts as a communication highway, linking the brain to vital organs and significantly modulating emotional responses. When the vagus nerve functions optimally, it helps regulate heart rate, digestion, and immune response, creating a calming effect that counteracts stress and emotional upheaval. Imagine the vagus nerve as a conductor, orchestrating a symphony of physiological processes that maintain balance and harmony within the body. Stimulating this nerve can enhance its regulatory functions, promoting calm and emotional stability.

To make these complex ideas more accessible, let's consider a simple analogy. Think of the vagus nerve as a thermostat for your body's stress response. Just as a thermostat maintains a comfortable temperature within a home, the vagus nerve helps keep your body's stress levels in check. When activated, it sends signals to slow the heart rate and encourage relaxation, like adjusting the thermostat to cool down a room on a hot day. This process illustrates how vagus nerve stimulation can bring about a state of equilibrium, reducing anxiety and promoting well-being.

Scientific evidence supports the efficacy of vagus nerve techniques, providing a solid foundation for their therapeutic use. A study published in the journal "Biological Psychiatry" demonstrated that individuals undergoing vagus nerve stimulation (VNS) experienced significant improvements in mood and emotional regulation. These findings underline the potential of VNS in alleviating symptoms of depression and anxiety, offering hope to those who have not found relief through traditional methods. Additionally, the FDA's approval of VNS devices for treatment-resistant depression and epilepsy further corroborates its effectiveness, highlighting its role in improving the quality of life for many individuals. Such endorsements from reputable sources lend credibility to the practice, encouraging further exploration and adoption.

Real-world applications of vagus nerve therapy abound, with numerous success stories illustrating its transformative impact. Consider the case of John, a veteran struggling with post-traumatic stress disorder (PTSD). After years of battling intrusive memories and emotional turmoil, John found respite through vagus nerve stimulation. By incorporating deep breathing exercises and mindfulness practices into his daily routine, he was able to activate his vagus nerve and reduce the intensity of his symptoms. Over time, John reported feeling more grounded and less reactive to triggers, demonstrating the tangible benefits of vagal engagement. His journey serves as a testament to the power of this therapy, inspiring others to explore its potential.

Despite its promise, vagus nerve therapy is not without its myths and misconceptions. One prevalent myth is that vagus nerve stimulation is a cure-all, capable of resolving any health issue with minimal effort. While VNS can be a powerful tool, it is most effective when integrated with a comprehensive approach to health, including lifestyle changes and other therapeutic interventions. It is essential to recognize that vagus nerve stimulation is not a standalone solution but a complementary practice that supports overall well-being. By dispelling these myths, we can cultivate a realistic understanding of what vagus nerve therapy can achieve, empowering you to make informed decisions about your health.

5.1 Ensuring Safety: Guidelines for Home Practices

Engaging with the vagus nerve through self-administered exercises opens up healing possibilities. Yet, a mindful approach is required to ensure safety, and this should be done by introducing these practices gradually. Much like a musical instrument, your body responds best when tuned gently. Start with short sessions and simple exercises, such as deep breathing or gentle humming, to familiarize yourself with how your body reacts. Pay attention to any sensations or feelings that arise, as these are your body's way of communicating its needs. As you enter a new workout regimen, allow your body time to adjust to these new experiences. By listening to your body's signals, you can tailor your practice to suit your unique needs, creating a safe and nurturing environment for healing.

As you explore these practices, be aware that mild side effects like dizziness or fatigue might occur. These responses are often temporary and can be mitigated by taking a break or adjusting the intensity of your practice. Imagine a gentle wave washing over you, signaling the need to pause and recalibrate. If you experience such sensations, return to your breath, grounding yourself in the present moment. However, it may be time to seek professional guidance if symptoms persist or intensify. Consulting a healthcare provider ensures that your practice remains supportive rather than overwhelming. They can offer insights and adjustments tailored to your health profile, helping you confidently navigate any challenges.

Knowing when to seek professional advice is crucial in maintaining a safe practice. If you encounter symptoms such as persistent dizziness, chest pain, or significant mood changes, you must contact a healthcare professional. These indicators suggest that your body requires additional support or that adjustments are necessary in your approach. Remember, reaching out for help is a proactive step in your healing journey, ensuring you are supported and informed. Healthcare professionals can provide reassurance and expertise, guiding you toward a practice that aligns with your health and well-being.

Creating a safe and inviting environment for your practice enhances safety and comfort. Choose a quiet, calm space to engage with your exercises without distractions. This space is your sanctuary, where you can retreat and focus inward. Consider incorporating elements that promote relaxation, such as soft lighting, soothing music, or a comfortable mat. These additions create an atmosphere conducive to healing, where your body and mind can unwind fully. By setting the stage for your practice, you allow yourself to engage more deeply, maximizing the benefits of each session.

Interactive Element: Creating Your Healing Space

Reflect on the elements that bring you peace and comfort. Consider how you can incorporate these into your practice environment. It could be a favorite chair, a gentle scent, or a cherished piece of art. Take a moment to visualize your ideal space and list items or adjustments that would enhance your practice. As you implement these changes, notice how they influence your experience, making note of any shifts in your journal. This reflection personalizes your practice and deepens your connection to the healing process.

5.2 Time Management:
Integrating Exercises into Daily Life

Incorporating vagus nerve exercises into a packed schedule can feel daunting, yet even the busiest days offer hidden pockets of time perfect for this practice. Imagine your day as a mosaic, each small segment with the potential for mindfulness and calmness. One practical approach is to designate specific windows for practice, treating them as essential as any meeting or appointment. First thing in the morning, when the world is still quiet, or before bed when the day's demands have eased. By setting aside these moments, you create a rhythm that supports your mental health and enriches your entire day with tranquility.

Even when time feels scarce, brief interludes can be transformative. Consider the minutes spent waiting for your morning coffee to brew or the lull between tasks at work. Often dismissed as inconsequential, these moments can become opportunities for quick breathing exercises or mindfulness practices. During commutes, for instance, try focusing on your breath, inhaling deeply through your nose, and exhaling slowly through your mouth. This simple exercise engages the vagus nerve and centers your mind, turning travel time into a serene escape. Similarly, a quick body scan or grounding exercise during a short work break can refresh your focus and energy, making these practices adaptable to the ebb and flow of daily life.

Prioritizing your mental health is more than a commitment; it's necessary. The benefits of regular vagus nerve engagement extend beyond immediate calm, fostering long-term well-being and resilience. Integrating these practices into your routine emphasizes self-care's importance as you schedule time for physical exercise. By consistently engaging the vagus nerve, you enhance your capacity to manage stress, cultivate emotional regulation, and improve overall mental health. This investment in yourself is not a luxury; it's a foundation for thriving amidst the pressures of modern life.

Time-related barriers often stem from perceptions rather than reality. To overcome these challenges, begin by identifying areas where procrastination may arise. Is it the overwhelming nature of starting something new or the belief that more pressing matters take precedence? By acknowledging these barriers, you can address them directly. Techniques such as breaking exercises into smaller, manageable steps or setting specific, achievable goals can reduce the tendency to delay.

Additionally, pairing vagus nerve practices with existing habits creates a seamless integration. For example, practice deep breathing while waiting for an elevator or perform a quick mindfulness check-in at a stoplight. These micro-interventions save time and weave moments of peace into the fabric of your day.

Incorporating vagus nerve exercises into your daily routine creates a tapestry of mindfulness that enriches each moment. Whether through designated times, opportunistic breaks, or integrated habits, these practices become a natural part of your life. Embracing this approach enhances your mental health and cultivates a sense of balance and ease, empowering you to navigate life's challenges with grace and resilience.

5.3 Avoiding Re-Traumatization: Safe Exploration of Techniques

Engaging with somatic practices offers a profound opportunity for healing, yet it comes with the risk of re-traumatization, a concern that warrants careful attention. Imagine opening a door into a room filled with memories—some comforting, others unsettling. In these moments, triggering sensations or emotions can arise unexpectedly, pulling you back into past experiences. This is where awareness becomes your ally. By tuning into your body's signals, you can carefully navigate these memories, recognizing the subtle cues that indicate when a practice might be too intense. Listening to your body's whispers helps you modulate your engagement, allowing for a gentle exploration rather than an overwhelming encounter.

To ensure a safe exploration of somatic techniques, begin with gradual exposure, akin to dipping a toe into a pool before fully immersing yourself. Start with practices that evoke mild responses and slowly increase the intensity as you build confidence and resilience. This approach allows your nervous system to acclimate, reducing the likelihood of being overwhelmed. Alongside this, grounding techniques serve as an anchor, keeping you rooted in the present moment. Whether it's feeling the texture of a surface under your fingertips or focusing on the rhythm of your breath, these techniques offer a lifeline when emotions surge. They act as a tether, preventing you from being swept away by the currents of past traumas.

Identifying and managing triggers is another critical component of safe practice. Triggers can be elusive, lurking in sensations, sights, or sounds. Keeping a journal can be an invaluable tool in this endeavor. By documenting your emotional responses during and after exercises, you map your experience, highlighting patterns and pinpointing specific triggers. This reflective practice enhances self-awareness and empowers you to make informed choices about your practice. With each entry, you gain clarity, enabling you to anticipate and navigate potential challenges more easily. This proactive approach transforms triggers from stumbling blocks into stepping stones along your path to healing.

In some cases, the insights gained from self-exploration indicate the need for professional support. Therapy or counseling can provide a haven where you can process difficult emotions with the guidance of a trained professional. Situations where strong emotional responses persist or where trauma feels too overwhelming to manage alone are clear indicators that additional support may be beneficial. A therapist can offer a structured space to explore these feelings, equipping you with strategies to navigate them safely. They can also help integrate somatic practices into your therapeutic journey, ensuring your approach is holistic and supportive.

Consider the value of a collaborative effort in your healing process. While self-guided exploration has its place, the expertise of mental health professionals adds a layer of safety and insight that can be invaluable. Their guidance can help you navigate the complexities of trauma, ensuring that your engagement with somatic practices is not only safe but also profoundly transformative. In this partnership, you find the balance between self-exploration and professional support, creating a pathway to healing that honors both your autonomy and your need for connection.

5.4 Consistency vs. Motivation: Building a Sustainable Routine

Creating a sustainable routine for vagus nerve exercises involves more than occasional practice; it requires dedication and a consistent approach. Think of it as building a foundation where you lay another brick daily, steadily constructing a solid structure supporting your mental and emotional well-being. Consistency is the key to unlocking lasting results. By incorporating exercises into your daily routine, you cultivate a deeper connection with your body and mind. Developing a habit around these practices can transform vagus nerve stimulation from a temporary relief into a lasting change. Establishing a daily routine might initially seem daunting, but it becomes achievable when broken down into manageable steps. Begin by selecting specific times each day to engage in your chosen exercises, whether during a morning ritual or a quiet moment before bed. This regularity reinforces the practice and signals your body that it's time to relax and reset.

Maintaining motivation over time might present a challenge, yet setting realistic goals can help keep your focus sharp and your commitment strong. Start with small, attainable milestones that allow you to track your progress and celebrate achievements. Your goal is to practice deep breathing each evening for a week. Once accomplished, recognize this success and set a new goal, gradually increasing the complexity or duration of your exercises. Celebrating these small wins reinforces positive behavior and provides a sense of accomplishment, fueling your drive to continue. Motivation can also be bolstered by aligning your practice with personal values or aspirations. Reflect on what truly matters to you—reducing anxiety, improving emotional regulation, or fostering a sense of peace—and let these motivations guide your practice.

To support your routine and maintain consistency, consider utilizing tools and resources that aid in habit formation. Habit-tracking apps or journals can be particularly effective in this regard. By documenting your practice, you create a visual representation of your commitment, allowing you to see patterns and identify areas for improvement. These tools gently remind you of your goals, providing accountability and encouragement. Additionally, integrating social support into your routine can enhance motivation. Sharing your progress with a friend or joining a community of like-minded individuals can foster a sense of connection and shared purpose, making the journey feel less solitary.

Despite best intentions, motivational obstacles may arise, and setbacks can occur. It's essential to approach these challenges with compassion and resilience. When progress stalls or motivation wanes, remind yourself of the reasons you began this journey. Revisit your goals and consider adjusting them if necessary, ensuring they remain relevant and attainable. Strategies for overcoming these barriers include breaking exercises into smaller, more manageable steps or simply revisiting the foundational practices that initially sparked your interest. Remember that setbacks are not failures but opportunities for growth and learning. Embrace them as part of the process, and use them to refine your approach, ultimately strengthening your commitment to a sustainable routine.

5.5 Overcoming Initial Hurdles: Early Challenges in Practice

Starting vagus nerve exercises can feel overwhelming, like stepping into a new world where everything seems unfamiliar. Many beginners face the challenge of establishing a consistent routine, finding it difficult to integrate these practices into daily life. It's common to feel discomfort with new exercises as your body adjusts to unfamiliar sensations and movements. This initial phase can be daunting, but recognizing these hurdles as natural parts of the process is crucial. Like an intricate instrument, the body requires patience as it adapts to new rhythms and practices. Often, the hardest part is simply beginning and allowing yourself to embrace the learning curve with an open mind.

To ease into vagus nerve practices, consider starting with more straightforward exercises that require less time and commitment. These could include short breathing exercises or gentle humming, which are accessible and easily incorporated into even the busiest schedules. As your confidence grows, gradually increase the complexity and duration of your practices. Think of it as building a foundation where each small step strengthens and prepares you for more advanced exercises. This gradual approach helps cultivate familiarity and comfort, allowing your body and mind to adapt at a manageable pace. It's like learning to swim in shallow waters before venturing into deeper depths, ensuring you feel secure and supported throughout the journey.

Patience and persistence are your greatest allies during this phase. It's important to remember that improvement takes time, and each practice session contributes to your progress, even if the changes aren't immediately noticeable. Reflecting on past experiences can be illuminating. For instance, consider the story of Rachel, who initially struggled with maintaining a routine. She began with three-minute breathing exercises each morning, gradually extending the time as she became more confident. Over several weeks, she noticed a subtle yet profound shift in her emotional resilience and stress levels. Her story is a testament to consistency and perseverance, illustrating that even small, incremental changes can lead to significant improvements.

Inspiration can also be found in the experiences of others who have persisted through early challenges. Take the example of Mike, who faced discomfort with new exercises, initially feeling awkward and unsure. However, he decided to continue, focusing on the positive shifts he began to notice, such as improved mood and reduced anxiety. Over time, these small victories fueled his motivation, encouraging him to explore more complex practices. Mike's journey highlights the importance of staying committed, even when uncertain or uncomfortable. By embracing the process and celebrating each small success, you can build a sustainable routine that supports your mental and emotional well-being.

As we conclude this chapter, it's clear that while the path to integrating vagus nerve practices may have challenges, it also offers immense rewards. With patience, persistence, and a willingness to start small, you can overcome initial hurdles and create a meaningful practice that enhances your well-being. This foundational work sets the stage for deeper exploration and integration, leading us into the next chapter, where we delve into more advanced techniques and their applications in everyday life.

Chapter 6:

SELF-EVALUATION AND PROGRESS TRACKING

Picture a sailor navigating the open sea, relying on the stars to guide their journey. Much like this navigator, you embark on self-discovery and healing, using self-assessment as your compass. Understanding your body's signals and responses is pivotal in charting a course toward well-being. You can gain insight into your body's resilience and adaptability by tuning in and measuring your vagal tone. This chapter introduces practical tools and techniques to help you gauge your vagal tone effectively, providing a foundation for personal growth and empowerment.

Heart rate variability (HRV) is a primary indicator of vagal tone and overall autonomic nervous system health. HRV measures variations in the time interval between heartbeats, reflecting your body's ability to adapt to stress. A higher HRV indicates a relaxed and resilient state, suggesting robust vagal tone and efficient parasympathetic function. Conversely, a lower HRV may signal stress or health issues. By monitoring your HRV, you can gain valuable insights into your physiological state and adjust your practices accordingly. Technological advancements make HRV measurement more accessible, with wearable devices and apps providing real-time feedback.

To assess your HRV, consider investing in a heart rate monitor or a wearable device designed for this purpose. These devices often sync with smartphone apps, offering detailed insights into your heart rate patterns and variability. To set up your monitor, ensure it's securely positioned on your body and follow the manufacturer's instructions for synchronization. Once connected, spend a few minutes in a relaxed, seated position, allowing the device to record your baseline HRV. Over time, you'll accumulate valuable data that can guide your self-assessment journey.

Another effective method for assessing vagal tone involves simple at-home breathing tests. By observing your body's response to controlled breathing exercises, you can glean insights into your autonomic balance. Begin by sitting comfortably, placing one hand on your chest and the other on your abdomen. Inhale deeply through your nose for a count of four, feeling your abdomen rise more than your chest. Hold your breath for a count of four, then exhale through your mouth for a count of eight. As you repeat this cycle, notice any changes in your heart rate or sense of relaxation. This exercise engages the vagus nerve and provides a tangible measure of your body's response to stress reduction techniques.

Regular self-assessment is crucial in tracking progress and guiding therapy adjustments. Establishing a weekly or bi-weekly assessment schedule can help you monitor changes in your vagal tone over time. By consistently evaluating your HRV and physiological responses, you can identify patterns and trends, allowing you to fine-tune your practices for optimal results. This continuous feedback loop empowers you to make informed decisions about your self-care and healing journey.

Interpreting your self-assessment results is an essential step in understanding your progress. When reviewing your HRV data, consider comparing your readings to standard benchmarks for your age and fitness level. A higher HRV indicates effective stress management and a balanced autonomic system. If your readings fall below these benchmarks, explore potential adjustments to your lifestyle and practices, such as incorporating more relaxation exercises or modifying your daily routine. By maintaining an open mind and embracing experimentation, you can discover what works best for you.

Reflective Exercise: Creating Your Self-Assessment Plan

Take a moment to reflect on your motivations for self-assessment and the goals you hope to achieve. Consider the tools and techniques you'd like to incorporate, such as HRV monitoring or controlled breathing exercises. Create a plan outlining your assessment schedule, including specific times and dates for evaluation. Record your initial readings and observations in a journal or app, noting any patterns or insights. This exercise serves as a roadmap, guiding your self-assessment journey and supporting your commitment to personal growth and well-being.

6.1 Emotional and Physical Symptom Tracking

Imagine a painter creating a vibrant landscape, each brushstroke contributing to the whole picture. Similarly, tracking your emotional and physical symptoms can reveal the broader landscape of your well-being. By meticulously observing patterns, you can uncover the intricate links between your symptoms and vagal tone. This process heightens your awareness and empowers you to make informed choices about your mental health. When you track symptoms such as anxiety levels, sleep quality, and digestive health, you gain valuable insights into how your body responds to various stressors. This information can guide you in fine-tuning your healing practices.

Setting up a symptom-tracking system is akin to laying the foundation for a sturdy house. Begin by choosing a method that resonates with you—a traditional journal, a digital app, or a combination of both. The key is to ensure that your preferred method is accessible and easy to integrate into your daily routine. As you embark on this endeavor, consider categorizing your symptoms into emotional and physical domains. Emotional symptoms might include feelings of anxiety, sadness, or irritability, while physical symptoms could encompass fatigue, digestive issues, or headaches. Delineating these categories creates a structured framework for observing patterns and trends.

Consistent tracking allows you to identify correlations between stressors and symptom flare-ups. For instance, you may notice that your anxiety intensifies during periods of sleep deprivation or that digestive discomfort coincides with stressful events. Recognizing these connections empowers you to take proactive steps in managing your well-being. If certain situations trigger increased symptoms, consider implementing relaxation techniques or adjusting your schedule to minimize their impact. Over time, this practice fosters a deeper understanding of your body's unique rhythms and responses, enabling you to navigate challenges with resilience and grace.

In your symptom-tracking journey, specific variables can serve as guiding stars. Consider noting your anxiety levels on a scale from one to ten, reflecting on how they fluctuate throughout the day. Monitor your sleep quality by recording your sleep hours and any disruptions during the night. Additionally, it tracks digestive health, noting instances of discomfort or irregularity. These variables, while diverse, collectively contribute to a comprehensive picture of your overall well-being. As you gather this data, patterns may emerge, illuminating areas that require attention or celebration. This process enhances self-awareness and provides a tangible measure of progress.

Interactive Element: Creating Your Symptom Tracking Chart

Create a personalized symptom-tracking chart to organize your observations. Divide the chart into sections for emotional and physical symptoms, and list relevant variables within each category. Dedicate a column for recording daily entries, and reserve space for notes or reflections. This visual representation of your data can be a powerful tool for spotting trends and identifying triggers. Consider adding colors or symbols to highlight significant changes or milestones as you interact with your chart. This creative approach makes tracking more engaging and deepens your connection to the insights it provides.

Tracking symptoms is a dynamic process that evolves. It requires patience and dedication, yet the rewards are substantial. By engaging in this practice, you cultivate a deeper relationship with yourself and your body, fostering a sense of empowerment and agency. As you continue to explore the connections between your symptoms and vagal tone, remember that each entry is a step toward greater understanding and wellness. Through this ongoing dialogue with your body, you pave the way for meaningful change and growth.

6.2 Setting Goals: Personalizing Your Healing Path

Imagine the clarity of standing on a mountain peak, the horizon stretching wide before you, each step you took to get there having been guided by clear goals. In therapy, setting goals serves a similar purpose, anchoring you with direction and intent. Clear goals are not just tasks to complete; they are beacons illuminating your path, enhancing focus and motivation as you work toward healing. When you define your aim, you create a roadmap that helps keep you on track, even when the terrain becomes challenging. This clarity fosters a sense of accountability, as each goal is your commitment. As you progress, these goals become milestones, celebrating each step forward and reinforcing your resolve.

Creating SMART goals can transform vague aspirations into actionable steps. This framework—Specific, Measurable, Achievable, Relevant, and Time-bound—ensures that each goal is well-defined and attainable. Specificity details precisely what you want to achieve, leaving no room for ambiguity. Measurable goals let you track progress, turning abstract concepts into tangible results. Achievability ensures your goals are realistic, given your resources and constraints. Relevance ties your goals to your broader objectives, ensuring they align with your healing vision. Finally, setting a timeline provides urgency, encouraging consistent action. For instance, if you aim to improve vagal tone, you might set a goal to enhance it by a certain percentage over three months, using HRV as a measure.

Flexibility is vital in goal-setting, as life is seldom predictable. Your goals should be adaptable, allowing for recalibration as you evolve. Revisiting your goals periodically helps you reflect on progress and make necessary adjustments. This process is not about abandoning your goals but refining them in light of new insights and experiences. You initially set a goal to reduce panic attack frequency by half within six months. As you progress, you may find that the timeline needs an extension or that additional support is beneficial. Flexibility ensures your goals remain relevant and achievable, fostering a sense of empowerment rather than frustration.

Consider potential goals for vagal nerve therapy that could inspire your objectives. Enhancing vagal tone by a specific HRV percentage provides a concrete target, encouraging consistency in practices like meditation or breathwork. Reducing panic attack frequency by half offers a clear focus, motivating you to integrate calming techniques into daily life. These goals, while specific, are also adaptable, allowing for growth and change. By setting such goals, you create a structured approach to healing that acknowledges both your current state and your potential. This dynamic process supports your mental health journey and cultivates resilience and self-efficacy.

Goal-setting in therapy is more than a planning exercise; it's a commitment to personal development and healing. As you craft your goals, think of them as stepping stones guiding you toward a future of well-being and balance. This structured approach encourages you to focus, adapt, and persevere, transforming challenges into opportunities for growth.

6.3 Journaling for Insight and Progress

Imagine sitting in a quiet corner, pen in hand, capturing the whirlwind of thoughts and emotions that swirl within. Journaling offers a sanctuary for introspection, a space to explore your inner world without judgment. Putting pen to paper allows for a dialogue with oneself, fostering self-discovery and healing. As you write, you deepen your understanding of your emotional landscape, uncovering patterns and insights that might have otherwise remained hidden. Journaling can be a powerful tool for increasing self-awareness, helping you recognize emotional triggers, identify recurring thought patterns, and track your progress.

To make the most of your journaling practice, consider incorporating structured prompts that guide your reflections. Daily reflection prompts can serve as gentle nudges, encouraging you to explore specific aspects of your experience. You might begin with questions like, "What emotions did I feel most strongly today?" or "What events triggered a significant emotional response?" These prompts invite you to delve into your emotional world, providing a framework for understanding how your experiences shape your feelings. Techniques for exploring emotional responses can also include free writing, allowing your thoughts to flow unfiltered onto the page, or creating mind maps that visually represent the connections between your emotions and experiences.

As you engage with your journal, it becomes a living document of your growth and transformation. By comparing past and present entries, you can witness your evolution, noting shifts in perspective, emotional resilience, and mental clarity. This reflective process highlights your progress and reinforces your commitment to healing. When you encounter challenging periods, revisiting earlier entries can provide reassurance and remind you of the strides you've made. Over time, your journal becomes a testament to your journey, capturing the struggles and triumphs that define your path to well-being.

Consider the story of a reader who discovered profound insights through her journaling practice. By consistently recording her thoughts and feelings, she noticed patterns in her emotional responses, particularly about specific stressors. These patterns revealed underlying triggers that fueled her anxiety and depression. With this awareness, she could effectively implement targeted strategies to manage these triggers. Her journal served as a mirror, reflecting the intricate dance between her emotions and experiences, empowering her to navigate her mental health with greater understanding and agency.

Journaling Prompt: Exploring Emotional Triggers

Set aside time each day to reflect on your emotional landscape. Use the prompt, "What events or situations today triggered a strong emotional response?" to guide your exploration. Write freely, allowing your thoughts and feelings to spill onto the page. As you review your entries over time, notice any patterns or recurring themes. Use these insights to inform your strategies for managing emotional triggers and enhancing your well-being.

6.4 Technology Aids: Apps and Devices for Vagal Monitoring

In today's digital age, technology has become an indispensable ally in the quest for improved health and well-being. Several innovative apps and devices offer real-time insights and convenience regarding monitoring vagal tone. Heart rate variability (HRV) apps stand out as powerful tools. They allow you to track subtle fluctuations in your heart's rhythm, providing a window into your autonomic nervous system's balance. These apps often come with user-friendly interfaces, making it easy to visualize your HRV data and observe trends over time. In addition to apps, wearable devices, such as smartwatches and fitness trackers, provide continuous monitoring capabilities. These devices can seamlessly integrate into your daily routine, offering constant feedback on your physiological state. By wearing one, you can monitor your body's responses throughout the day, whether at rest, exercising, or managing stress.

The benefits of using technology in self-evaluation extend beyond convenience. Real-time feedback allows for immediate adjustments, fostering a proactive approach to well-being. Imagine noticing a dip in your HRV while at work; this insight can prompt you to take a moment for deep breathing or a short walk, recalibrating your nervous system before stress accumulates. Furthermore, the accuracy offered by these technological aids enhances the reliability of your self-assessments. Rather than relying solely on subjective feelings, you gain objective data to guide your practices and decisions. Data analysis features, often included in these apps, allow you to track changes over weeks and months, offering a comprehensive view of your progress. This ongoing feedback loop creates a dynamic relationship between you and your well-being, empowering you to tailor your practices to your evolving needs.

Selecting the right technology involves evaluating app features and compatibility with your lifestyle. Consider the aspects of HRV monitoring most vital to you—the depth of data analysis, user interface, or integration with other health apps. Some apps offer guided breathing exercises and stress management techniques, turning them into holistic wellness platforms. Compatibility with your existing devices, such as smartphones or tablets, is also crucial. Ensuring the app or device syncs seamlessly with your technology can prevent frustration and ensure consistent usage. It's worth exploring reviews and testimonials from other users to gauge overall satisfaction and effectiveness, providing a clearer picture of what you can expect.

User experiences and testimonials underscore the effectiveness of these technological aids. Take the story of Lisa, who struggled with anxiety and found clarity through a wearable device. She shared how tracking her HRV offered newfound self-awareness, highlighting the impact of stress on her body. With this insight, Lisa became more attuned to her needs, implementing regular relaxation techniques and observing tangible improvements in her mental health. Her experience mirrors that of many others who have integrated technology into their wellness journeys, finding empowerment in the data-driven insights it offers. These stories remind you of technology's transformative potential, guiding you toward a deeper understanding of your body's signals and responses.

As you explore the world of technology aids for vagal monitoring, remember that these tools are not replacements for intuition or self-awareness. Instead, they complement your journey by providing additional insight and precision. Embrace their possibilities and allow the data to inspire curiosity and growth. Through the harmonious blend of technology and mindfulness, you cultivate a well-rounded approach to self-care that honors both the wisdom of your body and the innovations of the modern world.

6.5 Celebrating Milestones: Recognizing Progress and Success

Imagine standing at the edge of a cliff, looking at a view you've worked tirelessly to reach. Each step and climb has brought you here; the view is your reward. Celebrating milestones serves a similar purpose in the context of self-improvement and therapy. It offers you a moment to pause and reflect, reinforcing your progress. Recognizing these achievements is not merely about marking time; it's a vital practice that boosts motivation and self-esteem. When you celebrate your progress, you acknowledge the effort behind each step forward, solidifying your commitment and encouraging further growth. This recognition transforms your journey from a series of tasks into a narrative of triumphs, fostering a deeper connection to your goals and the personal growth they represent.

Celebrating personal milestones can take many forms, and creativity can enhance the experience. Consider establishing a reward system for achieving specific goals. Whether treating yourself to a favorite meal or indulging in a day of relaxation, these rewards serve as tangible acknowledgments of your hard work. Sharing your progress with supportive communities, whether in person or online, can amplify the joy of achievement. You invite encouragement and inspiration by voicing your accomplishments, creating a ripple effect that strengthens your resolve. Celebrating in this way reinforces your success and builds a support network, fostering connections that can sustain motivation during challenging times.

Reflecting on personal growth is an integral part of recognizing success. This reflection allows you to reflect on where you started, appreciating how far you've come. Journaling about your achievements and the lessons learned along the way can deepen this introspection. As you write, you honor the struggles and victories that define your path, creating a narrative of resilience and transformation. This practice solidifies your progress and provides insight into the proven effective strategies guiding future endeavors. By weaving reflection into your routine, you cultivate a mindset that values growth and perseverance, empowering you to face new challenges confidently.

Examples of milestones to celebrate in the context of vagal nerve therapy are plentiful and varied. For instance, reaching a new baseline in HRV signifies a tangible improvement in your autonomic balance and resilience. This achievement reflects your dedication to practices like deep breathing and mindfulness, showcasing the impact of your efforts on your physiological well-being. Completing a month of consistent practice through meditation, yoga, or other techniques is another milestone worth celebrating. This consistency demonstrates your commitment to self-care and healing, reinforcing the habits that support your mental and emotional health. Each milestone, no matter how small, represents a step forward, a building block in the foundation of your well-being.

As we conclude this chapter, remember that celebrating milestones is more than a momentary acknowledgment. It's a practice that reinforces your journey, enhancing motivation and self-worth. By embracing these celebrations, you embed a sense of achievement into your narrative, empowering yourself to continue moving forward with purpose and resilience. In recognizing progress, you weave a tapestry of success and growth, laying the groundwork for future achievements. The next chapter will explore the real-life success stories illuminating the path of vagal nerve therapy, offering inspiration and insight into the transformative power of these practices.

Chapter 7:

REAL-LIFE SUCCESS STORIES

In the quiet of a sunlit afternoon, Sarah found herself sinking into a familiar armchair, the weight of anxiety pressing heavily on her chest. For years, Sarah had been caught in the relentless grip of chronic panic attacks that seemed to eclipse the vibrant life she once knew. These episodes arrived unbidden, leaving her breathless and disoriented as if a storm had swept through her mind. Despite trying various medications, she felt as if she were merely treading water, the waves of anxiety threatening to pull her under once again. Medication offered a temporary respite, but the underlying tension persisted, whispering its presence in the background of her daily activities.

Sarah's introduction to vagus nerve exercises came unexpectedly during a wellness workshop her friend had suggested. Initially skeptical, she sat through the sessions with a raised eyebrow, unsure what to expect. The concept of the vagus nerve—a seemingly invisible thread linking her mind and body—felt abstract and elusive. Yet, as the facilitator guided the group through simple breathing exercises, Sarah noticed a subtle shift, a quieting of the storm within. The skepticism began to wane, replaced by a tentative curiosity as she gradually accepted the possibility that these exercises could offer more than she had imagined.

Among the techniques introduced, diaphragmatic breathing stood out as a powerful ally. Each morning, Sarah would sit quietly, hands resting gently on her stomach, focusing on the rise and fall of her breath. This practice grounded her, anchoring her mind in the rhythm of the present moment. The breaths flowed slowly, deliberately, inviting a calm to wash over her. She also incorporated guided meditations that focused on activating the vagus nerve. These sessions became a sanctuary of peace, a refuge from the chaos that anxiety so often wrought. Through these practices, she learned to engage her body's natural relaxation response, discovering the profound impact of tuning into her breath.

The transformation in Sarah's mental health was both gradual and profound. As weeks turned into months, the frequency and intensity of her panic attacks decreased significantly. The once-relentless storm began to abate, replaced by a newfound sense of control over her emotional landscape. She noticed a growing confidence in her ability to manage anxiety without the sole reliance on medication. This empowerment extended beyond her mental state, influencing her interactions and relationships. Friends and family observed a vibrant shift, noting her increased presence and engagement with life.

Sarah's journey exemplifies the potential of vagus nerve exercises as a tool for healing and self-regulation. The practices she embraced offered her a lifeline, a way to navigate the turbulent waters of anxiety with grace and resilience. Her story is a testament to the body's capacity for healing, a reminder that within each of us lies the power to cultivate calm and restore balance. For those embarking on their path of healing, Sarah's experience offers hope and inspiration, a beacon lighting the way toward a life enriched by peace and presence.

Reflection Exercise: Your Calm Space

Take a moment to consider a space where you feel genuinely at ease. It could be a corner of your home, a natural spot, or even a mental sanctuary you create through imagination. Reflect on what makes this space calming and how you might incorporate elements of it into your daily routine. Consider journaling about the qualities that bring you peace and how to nurture them. Use this reflection to guide your practice of vagus nerve exercises, enhancing your journey toward emotional balance and resilience.

Healing from Depression: David's Path to Recovery

David's life had been a quiet tug-of-war, the grip of depression pulling him away from the vibrant life he once knew. Long-term depressive episodes took their toll on his career, slowly eroding his passion and drive. Meetings that once sparked excitement became daunting tasks, and the creativity that flowed so effortlessly seemed to dry up. He tried various therapies, each offering a glimmer of hope that soon dimmed, leaving him feeling more trapped than before. Traditional treatments, including medication and cognitive therapy, provided minimal relief. Instead of seeing progress, David felt like he was moving through life in a heavy fog. This persistent battle with depression left him questioning whether he would ever reclaim the joy that once colored his days.

It was a conversation with a mental health professional who introduced David to the potential of vagus nerve stimulation. At first, he was hesitant and skeptical, as past treatments hadn't brought the relief he sought. The professional explained the science behind the vagus nerve, describing it as a key player in regulating mood and physiological responses. David learned that stimulating this nerve might offer a new avenue for managing his depression. Though cautious, he explored this path, understanding that it could complement his treatment plan. The idea of a more holistic approach intrigued him, and with a tentative hope, he began incorporating specific vagal techniques into his routine.

Cold exposure emerged as an unexpected yet effective tool in David's practices. The concept was simple: brief exposure to cold water, whether through a brisk shower or a splash of cold water on the face, could activate the vagus nerve. The cold shock was initially startling, but he soon found it invigorating. This simple practice became a daily ritual, a moment of clarity amid mental fog. Alongside cold exposure, David discovered the power of sound healing and vibrational therapy. He attended sessions where the resonance of singing bowls enveloped him, their vibrations creating a symphony that seemed to cradle his weary spirit. These sessions offered more than relaxation; they allowed his mind to be quiet and his emotions to settle, a respite from the relentless drone of depressive thoughts.

The transformation in David's mental health was profound. As weeks turned into months, he noticed a subtle yet undeniable shift in his mood and energy levels. The heaviness that had been his constant companion began to lift, replaced by a growing lightness and clarity. David engaged with work again, his creativity rekindled, and his motivation restored. The hobbies that once brought him joy—painting, hiking, playing guitar—slowly re-entered his life, each activity infusing his days with renewed purpose. He laughed more, enjoying the simple pleasures that depression had once obscured.

Through these practices, David experienced a reconnection with himself, a rediscovery of resilience he thought was lost. His journey underscores the potential of vagal techniques as a beacon of hope in the landscape of mental health. David's story is a testament to the body's innate capacity for healing, a reminder that even in the depths of depression, a path to light and renewal exists. For those navigating similar struggles, his experience offers inspiration and a gentle invitation to explore the healing potential that resides within.

PTSD and Personal Triumph: Emily's Story

Emily's life had become a series of fragmented moments, each one haunted by echoes of a past trauma that refused to stay silent. Flashbacks would ambush her without warning, vivid and relentless, pulling her back into memories she desperately wished to escape. Her body responded with hyperarousal each time, leaving her heart pounding, her breath shallow, and her mind racing. This constant alertness took a toll on her ability to maintain relationships and hold steady employment. Friends and family noticed her withdrawal, a gradual retreat from the world that had once been her stage. Over time, the isolation deepened, casting a shadow over her daily life. The weight of PTSD was palpable, not just in her mind but in her very bones, a silent specter that dictated her existence.

It wasn't until she joined a trauma recovery program that Emily first learned about the potential of vagus nerve therapy. Encouraged by a support group that had become a lifeline, she explored this unfamiliar territory. The program introduced her to foreign and strangely intriguing concepts, like rediscovering a language she once knew. As she listened to the facilitators speak of the vagus nerve and its role in regulating the body's response to stress, a flicker of hope ignited within her. There was a path that offered more than just coping strategies; it promised a way to rewrite the narrative that trauma had so cruelly imposed.

Emily's journey through this new landscape began with somatic experiencing exercises, a therapeutic approach that emphasized the body's role in processing trauma. These exercises became a cornerstone of her recovery, offering a gentle yet profound way to release the pent-up tension that trauma had locked within her muscles. By focusing on bodily sensations and allowing them to surface without judgment, she learned to navigate the intricacies of her emotional responses. This embodied awareness became a tool for transformation, helping her reclaim a sense of agency over her own body. Alongside this, Emily embraced mindfulness-based stress reduction, cultivating present-moment awareness and fostering a sense of calm amidst the storm. She engaged her vagus nerve through meditation and deliberate breathing, gradually reshaping her physiological responses to stress.

The changes in Emily's life were nothing short of remarkable. As she continued to engage with these practices, she noticed a newfound ability to manage stress and navigate triggers with a grace that had once seemed unattainable. The hyperarousal that had dominated her existence began to wane, replaced by a steadiness that allowed her to breathe deeply and live more fully. Within her relationships, Emily reached out, reconnected with loved ones, and rebuilt bonds that trauma had threatened to sever. Professionally, she regained confidence, returning to the workforce with a resilience that surprised even her. Her journey was not without its challenges, but it was marked by triumphs that affirmed the power of the body to heal and the spirit to rise.

Emily's story is a testament to the potential of vagus nerve therapy as a beacon of hope and healing. Her experience underscores our capacity for renewal, even in adversity. For those navigating the complexities of PTSD, Emily's journey offers a roadmap to resilience, a reminder that healing is not only possible but achievable through intentional practice and the courage to embrace new paths.

Chronic Stress and Resilience: Mark's Transformation

Mark had always been known for his dedication, often described as the cornerstone of his high-pressure workplace. But over time, the demands of his job began to wear down his resilience. The relentless pace and constant deadlines fostered an environment where burnout became inevitable. Day after day, the stress mounted, manifesting in physical symptoms that Mark could no longer ignore. Headaches crept in like unwelcome guests, pounding relentlessly at his temples. Sleep, which once came quickly, now eluded him, leaving him tossing and turning long after midnight with insomnia shadowing his every step. His body was sending clear signals, yet the demands of his career left him feeling trapped in a cycle of stress without an obvious escape route.

The turning point arrived during a moment of quiet reflection, sparked by a book on somatic therapy that Mark had picked up almost on a whim. He had been searching for answers, seeking something beyond the traditional stress management strategies that seemed to offer only temporary relief. The book opened his eyes to the potential of the vagus nerve, describing it as a conduit for enhancing well-being and resilience. Intrigued by the promise of a more integrative approach, Mark delved deeper, eager to discover how these techniques could be woven into his life. A sense of cautious optimism gradually replaced his initial skepticism as he realized that the key to managing his stress might lie within him, waiting to be unlocked.

Among the tools that Mark embraced, biofeedback emerged as a particularly valuable ally. This method allowed him to monitor his body's responses in real-time, offering insights into how stress affected his autonomic nervous system and, by extension, his overall health. By measuring heart rate variability (HRV), Mark could visually observe how his body reacted to stressors and, more importantly, how it recovered. This tangible feedback empowered him to adjust, fostering a deeper connection with his body's signals. Mark incorporated mindful movement practices, such as Tai Chi, alongside biofeedback, into his routine. These gentle, flowing movements encouraged a meditative state, allowing him to engage the vagus nerve and promote relaxation. Through this practice, he discovered a profound sense of peace that transcended the chaos of his professional life.

As Mark continued integrating these techniques, the impact on his well-being became increasingly evident. The energy that had once been sapped by stress returned, revitalizing his personal and professional life. The headaches that plagued him diminished in frequency and intensity, and sleep slowly reclaimed its rightful place, offering him the rest his body so desperately needed. Improved sleep patterns came with a newfound clarity and focus, enabling Mark to approach his work with renewed vigor. He found himself navigating the demands of his job with a sense of balance that had previously eluded him. The burnout that once threatened to engulf him was replaced by a resilience that allowed him to thrive amidst pressure rather than merely survive.

Mark's story illustrates the transformative potential of vagus nerve techniques when faced with chronic stress. His commitment to exploring new avenues for managing stress brought about a profound shift in his physical health and overall quality of life. His practices offered more than a reprieve from stress; they provided a framework for sustainable well-being and resilience. For those grappling with similar challenges, Mark's experience offers a testament to the power of somatic techniques, a reminder that within the complexity of modern life, there exists a path to balance and vitality that is both accessible and profoundly effective.

Empowerment Through Self-Regulation: Lisa's Experience

Lisa's life often felt like a whirlwind, her emotions swirling unpredictably, leaving her trapped in a cycle of impulsivity and regret. Her history was punctuated by moments of intense emotional dysregulation, where reactions came swift and unbidden, sometimes surprising even herself. Relationships, both personal and professional, bore the brunt of this turmoil. They faltered under the strain of outbursts and miscommunications. Friends grew distant, unsure how to navigate the emotional tides that characterized Lisa's interactions. In her workplace, maintaining focus became a struggle. Her mind is often consumed by the chaos within, making it difficult to sustain a stable career path. These challenges painted a picture of isolation and frustration and fueled a desire for change. Lisa knew she needed a way to regain control and cultivate stability.

Her journey toward self-regulation began with a simple yet powerful motivation—a deep desire for self-empowerment and independence. Lisa longed to break free from the constraints of her emotional reactivity and navigate life calmly and purposefully. It was during a pivotal session with her therapist, who introduced her to the concept of vagal techniques, that Lisa found a path forward. Her therapist explained how engaging the vagus nerve could support emotional regulation, offering a bridge between her mind and body. Intrigued by the potential, Lisa embraced the guidance and was eager to explore these new tools. This introduction opened the door to a world where she could actively participate in her healing rather than passively enduring the storm within.

Among Lisa's practices, loving-kindness meditation became a cornerstone of her routine. This meditation, which involves directing warm and compassionate thoughts toward oneself and others, resonated deeply with her. Lisa carved out moments to practice daily, focusing on phrases that fostered empathy and kindness. She discovered that these sessions soothed her turbulent emotions and cultivated a sense of inner peace. The practice allowed her to slow down, pause before reacting, and choose her responses more mindfully. This newfound mindfulness extended beyond meditation, influencing her interactions and allowing her to approach relationships with more extraordinary patience and understanding.

In parallel, Lisa incorporated heart rate variability (HRV) biofeedback into her daily regimen. By monitoring her HRV, she gained real-time insights into her physiological responses, learning to recognize patterns and triggers contributing to her emotional dysregulation. This feedback empowered her to make informed adjustments, engaging in breathing exercises or meditation when she noticed her stress levels rising. Over time, Lisa became adept at using biofeedback as a tool for self-regulation, transforming it into a practice that reinforced her emotional resilience. This combination of meditation and biofeedback provided a framework that supported her growth, enabling her to cultivate a state of balance and stability.

The impact of these practices on Lisa's life was profound. As she continued to engage with the vagal techniques, she noticed a remarkable shift in her emotional resilience and stability. The impulsive behaviors that once dominated her interactions receded, replaced by a calm deliberation that allowed her to navigate challenges with poise. Once strained by volatility, relationships began to mend as Lisa approached them with newfound empathy and patience. Friends and colleagues marveled at her transformation, noting her increased presence and engagement. Lisa found herself reconnecting with those she cherished, rebuilding bonds that the tumult of her past had strained. Professionally, she experienced a resurgence of focus and motivation, enabling her to pursue her career goals with renewed vigor and confidence.

Lisa's story is a testament to the power of self-regulation and the potential for growth through intentional practice. Her journey highlights the transformative impact of engaging the vagus nerve, offering a path to empowerment and healing. By embracing these techniques, Lisa unlocked a sense of agency and independence, discovering that within her lay the capacity for profound change. Her experience is an inspiring reminder that the journey to self-regulation is possible and within reach for those willing to explore the hidden depths of their potential.

A Therapist's Perspective: Integrating Vagus Nerve Techniques

In the landscape of therapy, where the mind often takes center stage, the intersection with the body presents a compelling frontier. As a therapist with years of experience treating anxiety and trauma, I've always been drawn to approaches that consider the whole person. Traditional methods, while effective, sometimes leave gaps, particularly when the body holds onto stress that the mind has yet to release. My curiosity about holistic and integrative approaches led me to explore the vagus nerve's role in emotional regulation. This nerve's profound influence on our autonomic nervous system intrigued me. It offered a tangible connection between mental and physical health that traditional psychotherapy alone sometimes struggles to address. My journey into this realm began with a series of workshops and training sessions that deepened my understanding of how to incorporate vagal exercises into therapeutic practice.

The integration of these techniques into therapy was both innovative and intuitive. I started using vagal exercises as complementary tools in sessions, noticing how they enhanced traditional therapeutic processes. I observed significant shifts by teaching clients simple practices like deep, diaphragmatic breathing and mindful movement. These exercises helped clients regulate their nervous systems, creating a foundation of calm from which they could engage more deeply with cognitive and emotional work. Training and workshops gave me the skills to effectively guide clients in these practices, ensuring they felt supported and informed as they explored new techniques. It became clear that these exercises were not just add-ons but essential components of a comprehensive treatment plan.

One case that stands out involves a client who came to me with severe anxiety that had persisted despite various treatments. By incorporating vagus nerve techniques, we achieved a breakthrough. The client learned to use breathing exercises to calm their racing heart and racing thoughts, creating space for more profound therapeutic insights. Over time, their anxiety levels decreased significantly, and they reported feeling empowered and capable of managing their symptoms in a way that previously seemed unattainable. Another client, struggling with the aftermath of trauma, found solace in these practices. They described a newfound control over their emotions, realizing that their body could be a source of strength rather than fear. These stories are echoed in numerous testimonials, highlighting the profound impact of vagus nerve techniques in a therapeutic setting.

Reflecting on these successes, I see the broader implications for therapy. Vagus nerve techniques offer a powerful avenue for mental health treatment, not as a replacement for traditional methods but as a complement that enhances their effectiveness. There's a growing advocacy for broader adoption of these techniques in therapeutic settings, a call to embrace a more integrative approach that honors the mind-body connection. Therapists are responsible for continuing to explore and refine these methods, supporting ongoing research that can further validate and expand their use. The potential for vagus nerve techniques to transform mental health care is immense, offering pathways to healing that are both accessible and deeply resonant with the needs of those we serve.

In the next chapter, we will explore the future of vagus nerve therapy and its potential to revolutionize mental health treatment. The stories shared here illustrate the transformative power of these techniques in real-life scenarios. They serve as a testament to the resilience of the human spirit and the profound impact holistic approaches can have on our well-being. As we look forward, the possibilities for integrating these practices into everyday life continue to expand, promising a future where healing and growth are within reach for all who seek them.

Chapter 8:

THE FUTURE OF VAGUS NERVE THERAPY

Picture the vastness of the ocean, where each wave carries the potential to reshape the shoreline. This mirrors the current landscape of vagus nerve therapy, where recent breakthroughs and ongoing research promise to redefine our understanding of mental health treatment. As science delves deeper into the intricacies of the vagus nerve, new pathways and functions are emerging, shedding light on its profound capabilities. Recent studies have uncovered how this nerve influences our emotional well-being and significantly modulates our immune system. This revelation opens new avenues for treating unrelated conditions like metabolic disorders. By understanding the vagus nerve's ability to decrease pro-inflammatory cytokines through the cholinergic anti-inflammatory pathway, researchers are exploring its potential in reducing chronic inflammation, a common thread in many mental health disorders.

Interdisciplinary collaborations are at the forefront of these advancements. Neuroscientists, psychologists, and medical researchers holistically join forces to explore the vagus nerve's capabilities. This collective effort is crucial, as it allows for a comprehensive understanding of how the vagus nerve interacts with different systems within the body. Such partnerships combine expertise and create a symbiotic environment where each discipline informs and enhances the other. This is particularly evident in studies examining the nerve's influence on neurodegenerative diseases. By understanding the nerve's role in cognitive function, researchers are beginning to see how it might slow the progression of disorders like Parkinson's and Alzheimer's. This cross-disciplinary approach is vital for developing innovative therapies that address the root causes of these complex conditions.

The potential applications of vagus nerve stimulation extend beyond current practices, offering hope for those with conditions previously considered untreatable. Researchers are exploring its effects on metabolic disorders, recognizing the nerve's ability to impact the body's energy balance and glucose metabolism. By modulating these processes, vagus nerve stimulation could pave the way for new treatments for obesity and diabetes, conditions that often intersect with mental health issues. Exploring these new therapeutic areas signifies a shift towards a more integrated approach to health, recognizing the interconnectedness of physiological systems. As the understanding of the vagus nerve deepens, its applications continue to expand, offering new hope and innovative solutions.

Clinical trials are at the heart of validating these promising therapies. Ongoing studies are investigating novel stimulation techniques that aim to enhance the efficacy and accessibility of vagus nerve therapy. For instance, researchers are exploring transcutaneous methods that offer a non-invasive alternative to traditional vagus nerve stimulation. These trials assess the immediate effects and examine the long-term benefits of these interventions. By understanding the sustained impact of vagal stimulation, researchers hope to establish protocols that provide lasting relief for conditions such as generalized anxiety disorders and fibromyalgia. The insights gained from these trials are invaluable, as they lay the groundwork for refining and optimizing vagus nerve therapies.

8.1 Interactive Element: Reflective Journaling Prompt

Consider a moment when you felt a significant shift in your mental or physical well-being. Reflect on what might have contributed to this change. Could it have been a change in routine, a new practice, or perhaps an emerging understanding of how your body responds to stress? Use this reflection to explore how future advancements in vagus nerve therapy might further enhance your well-being. Write down any insights or thoughts on how these therapies could impact your life, fostering a deeper connection to your healing journey.

This ongoing research and exploration of the vagus nerve's capabilities mark an exciting era in mental health treatment. As new pathways are discovered and interdisciplinary collaborations flourish, the potential for innovative therapies continues to grow. By embracing these advancements, we are paving the way for a future where mental health care is more comprehensive, personalized, and effective. The journey of understanding the vagus nerve is far from over, and as science progresses, so does the promise of improved health and well-being for all.

8.2 Innovations in Vagal Stimulation Devices

Technological advancements are pushing boundaries in the vagal stimulation realm, offering new ways to interact with the vagus nerve. Among the most promising developments are non-invasive stimulation devices designed to be user-friendly and accessible. These devices can help individuals manage their health from the comfort of their homes. For example, transcutaneous vagus nerve stimulation (tVNS) devices employ electrodes placed on the skin, delivering gentle electrical impulses to activate the vagus nerve. This method eliminates the need for surgical procedures, making therapy more accessible for many people. The rise of these non-invasive options has not only increased accessibility but also broadened the reach of vagus nerve therapy to those who might have been hesitant about invasive techniques.

The miniaturization of implantable vagal stimulators is another exciting frontier, marking a shift towards more discreet and comfortable devices. Modern implantable devices are becoming smaller, enhancing patient comfort and reducing the procedure's invasiveness. These compact stimulators target specific vagal pathways precisely, allowing for more tailored treatments. This precision is crucial in maximizing therapeutic outcomes and minimizing side effects. Patients benefit from continuous, unobtrusive therapy that seamlessly integrates into their daily lives, making it easier to adhere to treatment regimens. The combination of non-invasive and miniaturized implantable devices presents a promising future where vagus nerve stimulation is practical and minimally disruptive.

Wearable technology is also pivotal in the evolution of vagus nerve therapies. Integrating vagal stimulation with innovative wearable devices opens up possibilities for continuous monitoring and real-time adjustments. Imagine a wearable device that tracks your physiological data and provides immediate feedback on your vagal tone, adjusting stimulation levels to optimize therapeutic effects. Such innovations allow personalized treatment plans that evolve with the individual's needs. The convenience of having a wearable device that monitors and manages therapy continuously enhances adherence and empowers users to take an active role in their health. This level of engagement fosters a deeper connection between the individual and their treatment, promoting long-term well-being.

Several pioneering companies and researchers are at the forefront of these innovations, driving the field forward with their groundbreaking work. Companies like LivaNova, PLC, and ElectroCore Medical LLC are in charge of developing state-of-the-art devices that redefine how we interact with the vagus nerve. These companies are pushing technological boundaries and setting new standards for patient care. Interviews with leading researchers and developers reveal a shared vision of making vagus nerve therapy more accessible and effective for all. Their dedication to innovation and patient-centric solutions highlights the transformative potential of vagus nerve technology. As these advancements unfold, the landscape of vagus nerve therapy will continue to evolve, offering new hope and possibilities for individuals seeking relief from trauma, anxiety, and depression.

8.3 The Role of Technology in Vagus Nerve Therapy

In today's rapidly evolving digital landscape, technology is becoming integral to therapeutic practices, and vagus nerve therapy is no exception. Imagine having access to guided vagal exercises right at your fingertips. Apps that provide step-by-step instructions on performing these exercises are now available, making it easier than ever to integrate them into your daily routine. These digital tools enhance therapeutic delivery by offering personalized guidance, allowing you to track your progress over time. Many apps include features that remind you to practice, track your heart rate variability (HRV), and suggest modifications based on your feedback. This personalized approach ensures that you always work at a challenging and beneficial level, providing an interactive experience that keeps you engaged and motivated.

Beyond apps, digital platforms are revolutionizing how we track and analyze treatment progress. These platforms offer comprehensive dashboards that compile data from various sources, including wearables and manual entries. Presenting this data visually helps you understand trends and patterns in your body's responses to therapy. This insight is invaluable for individuals and healthcare providers, allowing real-time adjustments to optimize the effectiveness of the treatment. For example, if a particular exercise consistently improves HRV, the platform can recommend incorporating it more frequently.

This data-driven approach ensures that your therapy evolves with your needs, promoting sustainable and long-term wellness.

Virtual reality (VR) is another exciting frontier in vagus nerve therapy. VR environments crafted for stress reduction immerse you in calming, serene landscapes that engage your senses and promote relaxation. Imagine standing on a virtual beach, feeling the cool breeze and hearing the gentle waves while practicing deep breathing exercises. This immersive experience enhances the effectiveness of vagal exercises by providing a multi-sensory environment that fosters a deeper state of relaxation. The potential of VR extends beyond relaxation, offering therapeutic interventions that can be used to simulate real-world scenarios. This can be particularly beneficial for individuals with anxiety, as it allows for exposure therapy in a controlled and supportive setting. By gradually confronting stressors in a virtual environment, you can build resilience and confidence, translating these skills into real-life situations.

Artificial intelligence (AI) is pivotal in personalizing vagus nerve treatments. By analyzing user data, AI can tailor interventions to your specific needs. This customization is achieved through analyzing patterns in your physiological and behavioral data, allowing AI to suggest modifications that enhance the effectiveness of your therapy. For instance, AI can recommend specific breathwork exercises based on your stress levels or suggest adjustments to your routine based on your progress. This level of personalization ensures that your therapy is always aligned with your goals, maximizing its benefits. AI-driven platforms also provide real-time feedback, offering insights and adjustments that keep you on track.

Real-world applications of these technologies are already demonstrating their potential. Case studies reveal how patients using technology-enhanced therapies have experienced significant improvements in their mental health. One patient, for example, credited a VR-based relaxation program with reducing their anxiety levels and improving their sleep quality. Another found that an AI-powered app helped them manage their stress more effectively by providing tailored recommendations and real-time feedback. Therapists, too, are embracing these digital tools, finding that they enhance therapeutic outcomes by offering new ways to engage and support clients. The integration of technology into vagus nerve therapy is reshaping how we approach mental health, offering innovative solutions that are both accessible and effective.

8.4 Community and Support: Building a Network for Healing

Imagine a warm, understanding room where people gather to share their stories, listen, and grow. This is the power of community in vagus nerve therapy, where the collective strength of a network fosters healing and growth. Being part of a community offers more than camaraderie; it provides a safe space for individuals to exchange experiences and encourage one another. Online forums and support groups have become invaluable, allowing individuals from diverse backgrounds to connect and share their healing journeys. These digital spaces offer anonymity and accessibility, making it easier for people to open up and receive support without geographical constraints. The conversations here often spark insights that might have remained hidden if faced alone, creating a tapestry of shared wisdom and resilience.

Local workshops and meetups further enrich this experience, bringing the virtual into the tangible. These gatherings allow individuals to practice vagus nerve exercises together, guided by experts who facilitate learning and connection. There's something profoundly reassuring about practicing alongside others, feeling the shared energy and support in the room. Such environments nurture a sense of belonging and collective empowerment, reinforcing that healing is not a solitary endeavor but a shared journey. These events often catalyze deeper bonds, turning acquaintances into trusted companions on the path to wellness. In these settings, participants can ask questions, receive immediate feedback, and witness firsthand the transformative power of community engagement.

Efforts to build supportive communities have gained momentum, focusing on creating inclusive and empowering environments for all. Community-based programs are springing up, designed to bring vagus nerve therapy to underrepresented groups and those who might not have access to traditional healthcare. Collaboration between practitioners and community leaders is crucial here, as it ensures that programs are culturally sensitive and tailored to the specific needs of each population. These initiatives aim to break down barriers and create a more equitable landscape for mental health support. These programs gain credibility and reach by involving local leaders, fostering trust, and encouraging participation from within the community. The ripple effect of such programs extends beyond individual healing, strengthening the community as a whole.

Finding and joining these supportive networks can seem daunting, but it need not be. Start by exploring online communities dedicated to vagus nerve therapy, where you can read about others' experiences and contribute your own. Look for forums with active participation and a welcoming atmosphere where newcomers are encouraged to engage. Check community centers or wellness clinics for workshops and meetups when seeking local groups. Many yoga studios and holistic health centers offer classes and events focused on somatic healing and vagus nerve exercises. Reaching out to facilitators or group leaders can provide insight into the group's dynamics and focus, helping you find a space that resonates with your needs.

Stories of individuals who have benefited from community support illustrate the transformative power of collective healing. Take, for example, the story of Ben, who struggled with anxiety and found himself isolated and overwhelmed. After joining an online support group, he discovered a network of individuals who understood his challenges and offered unwavering support. Through their shared experiences, Ben learned new coping strategies and found solace in knowing he was not alone. In another instance, a local workshop became a turning point for Maria, who had battled depression for years. The encouragement and understanding she encountered there reignited her hope and commitment to healing. These stories are not unique; they are echoed in communities worldwide, showcasing the profound impact of support networks on recovery and well-being.

8.5 Advocacy and Awareness: Promoting Vagus Nerve Knowledge

In the vast field of mental health therapy, the vagus nerve remains a misunderstood component. Lack of awareness often leads to misconceptions, creating barriers to acceptance and integration of vagus nerve therapy into mainstream practice. Many still view it as an abstract concept distant from everyday reality.

Yet, understanding the vagus nerve's function can significantly impact how we approach mental health. Educating the public is crucial. It's about breaking down complex ideas into relatable terms and explaining how this nerve can influence emotions and stress responses. When people understand the science behind the vagus nerve, they can better appreciate its role in promoting well-being. Overcoming misconceptions requires a concerted effort to disseminate accurate information, engaging the public in meaningful conversations about how the vagus nerve can be an ally in mental health.

Advocacy efforts are gaining momentum worldwide, with various campaigns and initiatives raising awareness about vagus nerve techniques. National and international organizations are stepping up to promote understanding through public awareness campaigns and educational events. These initiatives range from online webinars to in-person workshops, each designed to illuminate the benefits of vagus nerve therapy. Advocacy organizations are also working to influence public perception by collaborating with healthcare providers, ensuring accurate information reaches those most need it. By highlighting success stories and research findings, these organizations aim to shift the narrative, presenting vagus nerve therapy as a credible and effective treatment option. With increased visibility, the hope is to encourage more individuals to consider this therapy, fostering a broader acceptance of its potential benefits.

For individuals passionate about promoting vagus nerve knowledge, there are many ways to advocate for themselves and others. Sharing personal stories is a powerful tool for inspiring change. When individuals open up about their experiences with vagus nerve therapy, they humanize the science, making it relatable and accessible. These narratives can dispel myths and offer hope, showing that healing is possible through these techniques. Additionally, participating in advocacy groups provides a platform for collective action. Whether through local meetups or online forums, these groups are instrumental in driving awareness efforts. Individuals can amplify their voices by joining forces, ensuring the message reaches a broader audience. Advocacy is not just about raising awareness; it's about building a supportive community that champions mental health and well-being.

The impact of advocacy extends beyond individual understanding, influencing policy and healthcare integration. Successful advocacy can lead to policy changes incorporating vagus nerve therapy into standard treatment protocols, offering more comprehensive care options. For example, some regions have started to recognize vagus nerve stimulation as a viable treatment for conditions like depression and anxiety, integrating it into mental health services. These changes reflect a growing acknowledgment of the therapy's efficacy, paving the way for its inclusion in healthcare systems globally. Advocacy efforts also contribute to destigmatizing mental health treatments, fostering an environment where individuals feel empowered to seek help without fear of judgment. By advocating for the integration of vagus nerve therapy into standard care, we can help create a future where mental health support is more holistic and accessible.

8.6 Envisioning the Future: The Next Steps in Somatic Therapy

In the expanding healthcare landscape, somatic therapy stands poised to step into the limelight, merging its traditional roots with modern medicine. Imagine a world where somatic practices, once considered alternative, become integral to mainstream medical treatments. This shift is not merely about recognition but transformation, as the therapeutic modalities inspired by vagus nerve research continue evolving. New techniques are being developed that leverage our growing understanding of this nerve's intricate role in emotional and physiological regulation. These innovations promise to enhance traditional somatic therapies, offering more precise interventions that cater to individual needs.

Continued research and innovation in somatic therapy are vital. There is an ongoing need for funding and support to explore uncharted territories within this field. This exploration is not just a scientific endeavor but a collaborative one. Interdisciplinary partnerships can bridge gaps, allowing neuroscience, psychology, and physiology insights to inform and enrich somatic practices. Imagine teams combining their expertise to design reactive and proactive interventions, anticipating the body's needs and responding with tailored therapies. Such collaboration can lead to breakthroughs that redefine what is possible in healing trauma, anxiety, and depression.

As somatic therapies gain acceptance, their impact on mental health treatment paradigms could be profound. Today's Healthcare models are often segmented, focusing on specific symptoms rather than holistic well-being. The broader acceptance of somatic therapies could catalyze a shift towards integrated care, where mental and physical health are addressed in tandem. This holistic approach acknowledges that mental health cannot be separated from physical health; they are interwoven. By embracing this perspective, treatment plans can become more comprehensive, offering patients a pathway to recovery that honors the complexity of the human experience.

Looking ahead, the integration of vagus nerve therapy into mainstream mental health care could lead to significant improvements in patient outcomes. Imagine a scenario where individuals experiencing anxiety or depression have access to a range of therapeutic options, each designed to complement the other. Vagus nerve therapies could work alongside cognitive and behavioral interventions, enhancing their efficacy and offering a more robust framework for healing. This integration could also help reduce the stigma often associated with mental health treatments. By normalizing these therapies and incorporating them into standard care, we can foster an environment where seeking help is seen as a step towards health rather than a sign of weakness.

The future of somatic therapy is bright, filled with the promise of innovation and transformation. As these therapies continue to gain traction and acceptance, they could redefine how we approach not only mental health but the very nature of healing itself. The potential to improve the quality of life for countless individuals is immense, offering hope and healing where it is most needed. This is about treating symptoms and fostering resilience, understanding, and growth. As we stand on the brink of this new era, the possibilities are as vast as they are exciting.

Conclusion

As we end our journey exploring the transformative power of the vagus nerve, I want to reflect on the profound impact this knowledge can have on your life. Throughout these pages, we've delved into the intricacies of this remarkable nerve, uncovering its vital role in regulating our emotions, managing stress, and promoting overall well-being. The vagus nerve, often overlooked, is truly the unsung hero of our mental health.

The key learnings from this book are theoretical concepts and practical tools you can integrate into your daily life. From simple breathing exercises to more advanced techniques like cold exposure and sound therapy, you now have a comprehensive toolkit to stimulate your vagus nerve and enhance emotional resilience. Remember, these practices are about managing symptoms and empowering you to take control of your healing journey.

As you embark on this path of self-discovery and growth, I encourage you to approach these practices consistently and patiently. Like any skill, strengthening your vagal tone requires regular practice. Set aside time each day to engage in activities that nourish your vagus nerve, whether a few minutes of deep breathing or an entire mindful movement session. Celebrate your progress, no matter how small, and remain committed to your well-being.

You don't have to walk this path alone. Surrounding yourself with a supportive community can make all the difference in your journey. Connect with others exploring vagus nerve therapy through online forums, local meetups, or sharing your experiences with loved ones. Together, you can inspire and encourage each other, creating a network of healing and growth.

Stay curious and open to new possibilities as you continue on this journey. The field of vagus nerve therapy is constantly evolving, with researchers and practitioners uncovering new insights and techniques every day. Keep learning, stay informed, and be ready to adapt your practices as new knowledge emerges. The future of mental health care is bright, and you are now part of this exciting frontier.

Before we part ways, I am grateful for allowing me to join your journey. As someone who has witnessed firsthand the transformative power of vagus nerve therapy, both in my own life and the lives of countless others, I am honored to have shared this knowledge with you. This book has informed and inspired you to participate actively in your mental health and well-being.

Remember, your vagus nerve is a powerful ally in your emotional balance and resilience quest. Trust in its ability to guide you towards calm, connection, and inner strength. You have within you the capacity to heal, grow, and thrive. With the tools and knowledge you've gained, you can now navigate life's challenges with greater ease and grace.

So, take a deep breath, tune into your body, and let your vagus nerve be your guide. The journey ahead may have its ups and downs, but you have the resilience and the resources to meet each moment with presence and compassion. Believe in yourself, stay committed to your practice, and know you can heal and grow.

As you close this book and step forward into your new chapter, I invite you to carry these teachings with you, not as a burden but as a source of strength and inspiration. The power to transform your mental health lies within you; your vagus nerve is the key to unlocking that potential. Embrace this knowledge, share it with others, and never stop exploring the wonders of your mind-body connection.

With gratitude and hope, Tatiana

References

- *The Vagus Nerve (CN X) - Course - Functions*
  https://teachmeanatomy.info/head/cranial-nerves/vagus-nerve-cn-x/
- *Stephen W. Porges, PhD | Polyvagal Theory*
  https://www.stephenporges.com/
- *Methods of assessing vagus nerve activity and reflexes*
  https://pmc.ncbi.nlm.nih.gov/articles/PMC4322860/
- *Vagal tone and the physiological regulation of emotion*
  https://pubmed.ncbi.nlm.nih.gov/7984159/
- *Recognizing the role of the vagus nerve in depression from ...*
  https://pmc.ncbi.nlm.nih.gov/articles/PMC9685564/#:~:text=Notably%2C%20vagus%20nerve%20stimulation%20owns,contribute%20to%20pathogenesis%20of%20depression.
- *Interaction of the Vagus Nerve and Serotonin in the Gut– ...*
  https://pmc.ncbi.nlm.nih.gov/articles/PMC11818468/

- *Vagus Nerve Stimulation (VNS) and Treatment of Depression*
  https://pmc.ncbi.nlm.nih.gov/articles/PMC2990624/
- *Understanding PTSD From a Polyvagal Perspective*
  https://www.ifm.org/articles/understanding-ptsd-from-a-polyvagal-perspective#:~:text=Polyvagal%20theory%20emphasizes%20sociality%20as,threat%20and%20support%20mental%20health.
- *Diaphragmatic Breathing - Johns Hopkins Medicine*
  https://www.hopkinsmedicine.org/all-childrens-hospital/services/anesthesiology/pain-management/complimentary-pain-therapies/diaphragmatic-breathing#:~:text=This%20causes%20the%20heartrate%20to,(or%20sympathetic%20nervous%20system).
- *The Effects of Mindfulness and Meditation on Vagally ...*
  https://pmc.ncbi.nlm.nih.gov/articles/PMC8243562/
- *5 Poses for Vagus Nerve Regulation*
  https://www.clinicalyogainstitute.com/post/5-poses-for-vagus-nerve-regulation
- *Jumping into the Ice Bath Trend! Mental Health Benefits of ...*
  https://longevity.stanford.edu/lifestyle/2024/05/22/jumping-into-the-ice-bath-trend-mental-health-benefits-of-cold-water-immersion/
- *CBT Tips to Regulate the Nervous System*
  https://bayareacbtcenter.com/cbt-tips-to-regulate-the-nervous-system/

- *The Vagus Nerve: A Key Player in Your Health and Well-* ...
  https://www.massgeneral.org/news/article/vagus-nerve
- *Somatic Therapy To The Rescue Of The Vagus Nerve*
  https://www.atimetohealpsychotherapy.com/somatic-
  therapy-to-the-rescue-of-the-vagus-nerve
- *Stimulating the Vagus Nerve with HRV Biofeedback*
  https://blog.getlief.com/hrv-biofeedback-for-the-vagus-
  nerve/
- *Clinical perspectives on vagus nerve stimulation*
  https://pmc.ncbi.nlm.nih.gov/articles/PMC9093220/
- *Clinical perspectives on vagus nerve stimulation*
  https://pmc.ncbi.nlm.nih.gov/articles/PMC9093220/
- *Vagus nerve stimulation*
  https://www.mayoclinic.org/tests-procedures/vagus-
  nerve-stimulation/about/pac-20384565
- *Vagus Nerve Exercises: Heal Your Vagus Nerve Naturally*
  https://www.re-origin.com/articles/vagus-nerve-exercises
- *Polyvagal Self-Assessment*
  https://sacredpathholistictherapy.com/polyvagal-assessment/
- *Heart Rate Variability*
  https://documentinghope.com/heart-rate-variability/
- *5 SMART Therapy Goals For Anxiety - Set Effective* ...
  https://texascip.com/therapy-goals-for-anxiety-set-
  effective-treatment-goals/
- *The Power of Journaling for Mental Health*
  https://www.talkspace.com/blog/journaling-for-mental-health/

- *Bolster Your Brain by Stimulating the Vagus Nerve*
  https://www.cedars-sinai.org/blog/stimulating-the-vagus-
  nerve.html#:~:text=One%20way%20to%20activate%20
  the,for%20a%20count%20of%20eight.
- *Vagus nerve stimulation implant praised by depression ...*
  https://www.bbc.com/news/uk-england-
  leicestershire-52661277
- *Somatic Experiencing for Posttraumatic Stress Disorder*
  https://pmc.ncbi.nlm.nih.gov/articles/PMC5518443/
- *The Vagus Nerve: A Key Player in Your Health and Well- ...*
  https://www.massgeneral.org/news/article/vagus-nerve
- *Neuroimmunomodulation of vagus nerve stimulation and ...*
  https://www.frontiersin.org/journals/aging-neuroscience/
  articles/10.3389/fnagi.2023.1173987/full
- *Vagal Nerve Stimulation Companies*
  https://www.marketresearchfuture.com/reports/vagal-
  nerve-stimulation-market/companies
- *The Evolution of AI: A Game Changer in Mental Health and ...*
  https://www.rachelekraft.com/blog/the-evolution-of-ai-a-
  game-changer-in-mental-health-and-anxiety-management
- *Vagus Nerve Society*
  https://www.vnsociety.org/#:~:text=The%20
  Vagus%20Nerve%20Society%20is,spectrum%20of%20
  health%2Drelated%20conditions.

Made in the USA
Columbia, SC
07 April 2025

426f7729-5a7a-47a5-8a82-cb3a1959a70bR01